FROM DUNFERMLINE TO LONDON

About the Author

Jeanie Traynor Maltby (née Shaw) grew up in High Valley Field – a mining village in Scotland. Rejecting an office job, she embarked upon a career in nursing. She trained as a staff nurse in Edinburgh, with the NHS in its infancy, before a desire to widen her horizons took her to London.

FROM DUNFERMLINE TO LONDON

Memoirs of a Staff Nurse
1950–1962

Jeanie Traynor Maltby

Matador
9 Priory Business Park,
Wistow Road, Kibworth Beauchamp,
Leicestershire. LE8 0RX
Tel: 0116 279 2299
Email: books@troubador.co.uk
Web: www.troubador.co.uk/matador
Twitter: @matadorbooks

ISBN 978 178901 375 7

British Library Cataloguing in Publication Data.
A catalogue record for this book is available from the British Library.

Printed on FSC accredited paper
Printed and bound in Great Britain by 4edge Limited
Typeset in 11pt Minion Pro by Troubador Publishing Ltd, Leicester, UK

Matador is an imprint of Troubador Publishing Ltd

I dedicate this book to my mother, Martha, who put me on the right path to train as a nurse. I also thank my daughter Gillian who persevered in helping me with the publication process.

These memories of my nursing career are very special to me; I met wonderful nursing friends and amazing patients whom I remember as if I had met them yesterday. I had very happy times but also very sad moments in my nursing. I started in the NHS in infectious diseases, which was a three-year course to register as a "fever nurse", then "general", which was a two-year course to register as a "registered general nurse", and from there onto "maternity", which was another two years (which I didn't finish). I then went on to work in private nursing, where I met royalty, VIPs and celebrities. The NHS then drew me back in and I ended up as sister in charge of theatres.

I left school at fifteen in 1948, the year the NHS was created. I had a good education at a secondary school in a Scottish mining village. I had no idea what I wanted to do in life. I felt a little scared about finding a job but I knew I didn't want to work in a factory or a shop. I scanned the local press jobs vacancy section and noticed that an insurance firm in the town wanted an office girl and would pay £2.50 per week. I applied on the Saturday and started on the Monday. The office was small and dingy and smelled of gas. The boss, Mr Findlay, was a big, ruddy-faced man wearing a striped suit with waistcoat, watch, chain and a big cigar. A big Remington typewriter was on my desk; I told him I couldn't type. He said, "Don't worry about that; you will soon pick it up."

So I filed some papers, took dictation from Mr Findlay and plonked it out with two fingers on the typewriter. I'm sure this typewriter was second-hand. It was ancient and the letter H was crooked. When I think of the high-tech world today, I laugh at the letters I sent to the main office in London. The boss would be out most days, so it was a lonely existence sitting there twiddling my thumbs. I stayed for just over a year and then left. I hated the job even though Mr Findlay and the six insurance agents were very nice men – all quite elderly. The job was not for me.

I was at home, not knowing what I was going to do, when my mother said, "How would you like to be a nurse? I'm sure you would like it." Cathie Wallace, who lived in our village, was a nursing sister in one of the hospitals in town. My mother and I went down to ask her advice about the possibility of me taking up nursing. She encouraged me to apply, but also said it was hard work. She also said it was an infectious diseases hospital, but that didn't seem to worry me or my mother, because I wasn't different from any of the other girls that worked there. So I applied for a post as a probationer nurse. I got a reply from the matron two days later asking me to come in for an interview the next day. I suddenly felt sick in the stomach, but my mother soon calmed me down by saying, "If you don't like it, you can come home." In those days, nurses in training had to live in the nurses' home.

When I arrived at the hospital for my interview, I rang the gleaming big brass bell at the side of two thick polished wooden doors; they were so big a bus could have driven through them. A Miss Wilson, in navy blue uniform with a frilly white collar and stiff, frilly white hat, came to the door. She was tall and very slim, with sharp features, upright and as stiff as the hat on her head. I introduced myself, thinking she was the matron, but then she said, "Wait there. Matron will see you soon."

The door opened and this obese woman wearing a black dress and black stockings and shoes with short black hair filled the doorway. She said, "Come in, Miss Shaw. I am Miss Emslie, the matron; tell me a little about yourself." She then asked me if I was fit and well and willing to put my heart and soul into my work. She told me what she expected of her nurses, as well as the rules and regulations. She then told me to come into the next room to get measured for my uniform. I felt like telling her I had changed my mind but I was too scared. It was Friday and I was told to report for duties on Monday. I went home and told my parents I had been accepted and had just the weekend to pack. They were happy for me but I felt tearful because I thought I would be away from home for weeks and get homesick, but my mother said, "Jeanie, you are only six miles away and you do get time off." I felt more settled then and started to pack. I had butterflies in my stomach all through my packing and was shedding more tears – after all, I was leaving home and an unknown experience was looming that frightened me. I said all my goodbyes to friends, neighbours and family. My brother, Tom said, "You would think you were going to Timbuktu. It's only two short bus rides away!" Actually, he did make me feel better by saying that. I boarded the bus and arrived at the hospital at 9.00am. Miss Wilson opened the big doors again, welcomed me into the hall and informed me that she was both the assistant matron and home sister all in one (the home sister looked after all the nurses who lived-in). I wondered if she got two salaries! I was shown to my room, which I was to share with a nurse – Janet Henderson. The room was big and very pleasant with two beds made up with crisp white sheets, three blankets and a blue counterpane. My uniform, aprons and caps were lying neatly piled on my bed. Miss Wilson told me to unpack and then go down to the dining room at 11.00am for coffee or tea, where I would meet some of the nurses and my room-mate, Janet.

The dining room was large, with one long table down the middle with around ten chairs either side. A smaller table at the top of the room was for the sisters. I met Janet, who was very friendly and cheerful; she looked smart in her striped uniform and apron. Then she introduced me to Rena Dunn, Margaret MacLean, who was a bit of a comic, and Isobel Penman, who looked at me cross-eyed over her glasses and asked me which ward I was going to. Well, I didn't know at that stage but would no doubt be told the next morning.

After coffee, I went up to the sitting room and met two more nurses: Helen and Rose McGonagle, who were Irish sisters from Donegal. They were knitting and talking so fast I couldn't understand them. I felt a lot better having met some of my colleagues. I also got to know most of the "dos and don'ts" but was sure I wouldn't remember them all.

I didn't sleep well my first night. I felt strange, excited and cold – even though I had brought my hot water bottle. Suddenly, there was a loud knocking on the door and the night sister shouting, "Half past six, nurses!" I got up first and went out to wash. The bathroom was just outside our door. I thought how lucky I was to get there first, before all the others.

When I got back, Janet said, "Gosh! That was quick."

I said, "I know! I beat the others!"

Well, we got dressed but I had trouble making up my cap. Janet was still trying to master it herself – she had only been there one month. However, Rena Dunn came to the rescue. Rena had been there almost one year. When we went down to the dining room, Miss Wilson, the assistant matron, was seated at the top of the long table waiting to serve us with bacon and fried bread. We all had our allocated places at the table according to seniority. We all finished breakfast at the same time and stood up at the same time, with the newest nurse – yours truly – running to open the door to let all the others march out like soldiers. It was very military style. I was told to report to OB2 with Janet. So my first day on observation block 2 was about to begin.

We started our duties at 7.20am. I was first introduced to Staff

Nurse Ford. She looked very severe and strict, her hair pulled back in a bun, but very smart-looking. She took me on a tour of the cubicles, kitchen, bathroom and sluices. There were twenty cubicles upstairs and twenty downstairs. As it was an infectious diseases hospital, every patient had to be isolated in their own little room, which contained a bowl of disinfectant, a towel and two gowns. Nurses had to wash in the disinfectant before leaving the cubicle. At 8.00am the sister came on duty and called all the nurses to the office to give a report on the patients. We all stood in a circle with our hands behind our backs and after the report we were told what our duties were for the morning. The most senior nurse did all the important duties such as giving out medicines, injections, dressings and treatment. The babies had to be bathed and bottle-fed. All adults were given a bed bath once a week and pressure areas were treated twice daily. The junior nurses did most of the cleaning and making beds. Before all this started, the breakfasts were given out and very ill patients were fed. Janet and I were the most junior so I was sent to clean the bathrooms and the sluices, whilst Janet was sent to clean the treatment room.

Staff Nurse Ford was always keeping an eye on us, drawing her fingers along ledges looking for dust. 11.00am soon came round and that meant coffee. Janet and I were sent for our fifteen-minute coffee break with Staff Nurse Ford. Janet asked me when I was off but I hadn't been told my off-duty rota. However, Staff Nurse Ford said, "Oh you have a 4.30pm."

Well, I felt so happy I couldn't believe I would be off at that time and able to go home and see my parents. Oh, the coffee was very good, as were the two rich tea biscuits! Staff Nurse Ford had taken me under her wing. The first task I was to encounter was how to make a bed. Two chairs were put back to back at the foot of the bed and the bedclothes were folded neatly and placed over the chairs. It was the corners that got me: they had to be folded like an envelope and neatly tucked in, the pillows plumped up with openings away from the door. Making a bed with the patient in it was a different kettle of fish because the patient was rolled side to side and never exposed. I soon got the hang of bed making and, to this day, I have my hospital corners at home.

My next task as a junior was giving out and taking in bedpans and bottles. I gave out quite a few before I could master the washer and steriliser. On one occasion, I didn't close the door properly, pressed the lever and got drenched. I didn't make that mistake again! It was my first day and my feet were beginning to feel too big for my shoes. I must have walked miles and I was to find out later that we nurses covered about five miles per day. Oh, how I longed to get my feet into a hot bath! My mother and father were so pleased to see me that evening – it was questions all the time. They did laugh about the steriliser incident. It was so good being home for a few hours but I had to leave at 9.30pm, get the bus and be back at the hospital for 10.30pm, where the night sister would unlock the door to let me in. I did miss the bus on the odd occasion, which meant I arrived back later than 10.30pm; of course, this meant the night sister reported me to Matron and I had to be on the carpet the next morning. Matron told me off and said that it was not becoming of a nurse to be out late at night. So I always tried to catch the earlier bus.

I was beginning to settle into the hospital now and realising it was a serious vocation I had chosen. We had lectures from Dr Martin, Dr Wink and tutor Sister Horsley. I was beginning to understand how infectious these diseases were, but somehow I wasn't really scared because I didn't think I would ever catch anything. We were always lectured on the importance of hygiene such as daily baths and washing our hair often and keeping it short. Washing our hands on duty was an essential part of our training; it was stamped on our brain. I had wavy hair and it was getting a bit below my collar so I was called to the office and Matron said, "Nurse, you have very pretty hair, but you will need to get it cut." Well, I didn't feel too bad about that because I had been cutting my hair since I left school, so the next night I trimmed about two inches off my hair. I did go to a hairdresser once but never again: I looked like I had brown candyfloss stuck on my head!

Another taboo for us nurses was no make-up or jewellery, which meant no wristwatches, rings or earrings. We were allowed watches pinned to our top pocket; these were upside-down to take pulses. Alternatively, we had little metal egg timers with the sand running through for the half-minute. In terms of make-up, we were allowed a little face cream such as Ponds. No perfume was permitted. Well, even if it was, I could only afford Woolworth's Californian Poppy and if it were still around I would spray it all over me. I loved it – and not just me. Why do some lovely fragrances just fade away?

When I had been there for two or three days, I was still using the bathroom outside our bedroom. I said to Janet one morning, "Gosh, isn't it great that we are near the bathroom?"

Janet said, "You haven't been using that one, have you?"

I said, "Yes."

Then she informed me that it was Matron's and the assistant matron's. I didn't make that mistake again! The rest of the nurses thought it was a hoot, especially the Irish sisters. They said, "Oh, Jesus, Mary and Joseph," blessing themselves.

The main building was built of red brick. It was architecturally a beautiful structure. It looked rather like a stately home from one of Jane Austen's novels. The matron's, assistant matron's and nurses' rooms were all on the top floor. The matron dined in her own bedroom. The dining room, domestics, kitchen and dispensary were on the ground floor. A side door off the main building led to the wards via a covered gangway.

The "Scarlet" ward was directly opposite and divided into two big rooms: the left side, with cots, and right side, with beds, holding approximately thirty-two children. There was also a large kitchen and playroom with toys and a rocking horse. Going up the gangway 200 yards on the left was observation ward 1 (OB1). This was a single-storey ground-floor building with eight, three-bedded rooms. The twenty-four patients confined here had acute asthma, eczema and other skin conditions and included non-active TB patients who were convalescing. Going further up the covered gangway another 200 yards was OB2: a two-storey building. It had sixteen two-bedded cubicles on the ground floor. We also accommodated three cubicles for babies. A huge variety of diseases were nursed here, for example whooping cough, bronchial pneumonia, chickenpox, measles, meningitis, polio, croup, dysentery, mumps and typhoid.

Upstairs was exactly the same as downstairs but in these cubicles were the acute TB patients, fourteen males on the left and fourteen females on the right. We always kept two empty cubicles for any emergency, with the night sister's office in the middle. All these cubicles had glass partitions so that the nurses could observe the patients in the other cubicles too. The matron paid a visit to all the wards at 9.00am every morning. This was called "doing the rounds." We could see the matron coming up the gangway so whichever nurse was nearest the door opened it and said, "Good morning, Matron."

In fact, the film *Carry On Nurse* was a very true picture of our hospital and Hattie Jacques was not unlike our matron but without the make-up.

Having been there a month I got my first salary, £6.15. £4.00 went to my mother because, after all, she bought my clothes, shoes and toiletries. We were not allowed to go out in our uniforms, being an infectious diseases hospital. The £2.15 paid for the coffee shop, ballroom, cinema and black stockings. Matron never missed a ladder in your stockings: that was definitely not allowed. The nurses were a grand lot and we became more like a family. I went into town with a second-year nurse. She had to go to Boots for shampoo and she introduced me to the manager as another ID nurse. So from that point, I received 10% off in the shop. I told my mother that from then on I would buy all the toiletries myself. All the other girls did the same after I told them what Boots offered nurses. Boots eventually gave us a discount card with ID nurse on it. I was beginning to enjoy my life as a nurse and was asking more questions. We had a very good tutor, Sister Horsley. It was very hard work learning anatomy, physiology, hygiene and dietetics, plus the signs and symptoms of so many diseases and the treatments. I said to the tutor, "I'll never remember all these signs and symptoms."

And she said, "Oh you will when you come face-to-face with them." And that was very true. The children we treated with polio were heart-breaking: legs paralysed with wasting of the muscle. We didn't have physiotherapists in our hospital so the general hospital would send up one to instruct us as to what we had to do. It was all about exercise, massage and resplinting. It was very painful for the children to have this done morning and evening, but it had to be done and we didn't forget a little treat for them. Sister had a little jar of lollipops and – yes – we did have success at the end of their long stay. The children walked with callipers.

The experience of babies being admitted with whooping cough was a frightening one for me. When you hear a baby "whoop" it travels a long distance and that was when a nurse was allowed to run. But, no matter how fast you ran to that baby, when you got there you were looking at a little wax doll: lifeless. You could do nothing but wait until another whoop came with an intake of breath, then you would have to clear the airways with a fine suction tube and the little body turned red all over. You had to stay until the spasm episode was over, then the next one started. Recovery was when episodes became less frequent. I can honestly say we never lost a baby to whooping cough.

We did lose two babies with bronchial pneumonia and gastroenteritis. I dreaded babies coming in with these diseases.

They always looked so ill and you wondered if you were going to win or lose a helpless little babe. On one occasion we treated a baby with very bad croup. At six months he was fighting to breathe, with a croaking noise. The sister had the steam tent all rigged up over the cot, with the kettle pumping out steam. Well, it was like magic when we put this little body into the cot, because his breathing became easier and quieter in minutes. I knew then that he would be OK. The steam moistens the trachea and all the bronchi leading to the lungs. More or less the same thing happens if you have a dry mouth: a drink makes it feel better. I felt very sorry for the three- to five-year olds who came in with measles, German measles, mumps or chickenpox. These were all notifiable diseases because of the large families and the health authorities were trying to stop the spread. But the three- and five-year olds didn't understand why they couldn't see their parents for two weeks. Our hospital did not permit visitors; they could hand in "goodies" but they were not allowed in the wards.

Rosyth Dockyard was a very busy port. When a ship came in we were sure to get a few sailors in with mumps, chickenpox, dysentery or typhoid and sometimes just a fever of unknown origin – pyrexia of unknown origin (PUO). One day the medic on the ship rang up to report one sailor with smallpox. This meant red alert. The cubicle would be sealed off from all the others. Two nurses were chosen to nurse the patient with masks, gloves and special white boots and clothing – special everything for that one patient. We were all on edge, then we heard the siren of the ambulance coming up. Dr Wink was waiting to diagnose the patient in the ambulance and when he re-emerged he breathed a sigh of relief: it was a very bad attack of chickenpox. He was absolutely covered; the poor chap was very ill. We had to cover all the lesions with a sticky lotion to seal them, give penicillin, a sedative and a good diet and eventually he started to recover. Then we would allow a bath to get rid of all the crusted lesions. These patients were all confined to bed so they had to have bottles, bedpans and bed baths. They had to stay in their cubicles until they were discharged. Visitors were not permitted.

A high-ranking officer was admitted with mumps. He had a face like Desperate Dan in the Dandy. It's a serious business when an adult male gets mumps. They are very ill and not allowed to do anything. They are nursed lying flat, washed and fed for one week. The scrotum is laid on a raised soft cotton wool pad. This prevents orchiditis, which would render the patient sterile. When the swelling on his face subsided, wow! He had the looks of the actor Cary Grant – very handsome. He was allowed to sit up in bed after one week. All the nurses were crazy about him. I felt so embarrassed because he was just staring at me the whole time. I adjusted his cotton wool pad; he thanked me for making him feel comfortable and asked me to call him Tricker. I later found out from another sailor who was from the same ship that Tricker played tricks on his mates and put them in embarrassing situations – hence the nickname. Well he certainly tried to embarrass me every time I passed his cubicle. He would call out, "Nurse, my cotton wool pad has slipped!"

However, I got my own back on him. I sent in Nurse Colville to him and Betty was not as gentle as she should have been. Maybe it was because she was a farmer's daughter and had been used to handling bullocks on the farm. Anyway, Betty sorted him out! We didn't hear a squeak from Tricker anymore. He was quite a charmer. He did ask me to see him again when he was being discharged but I declined because I thought he was too handsome not to be married and he probably had a girl in every port. Not only that, I was eighteen years old and Tricker was thirty; my parents would not have approved.

By now nine months had passed and I was learning more skills: giving injections, medications and making up babies' bottles and feeding them. So now it was time for me to go on night duty, which was twelve-hour shifts for three months. I was going to be on duty with Staff Nurse Ford, who was an excellent nurse and a good worker. We had our light supper at 6.00pm, then I had to go to the kitchen to collect our food for our midnight meal. In the tray were four large potatoes, three eggs and two jam jars filled with soup – nearly always lentil. Some nights we would get cheese and four slices of bread. I did charm the cook into giving me enough fat to make chips when I had been on duty a week, so I carried the tray up to the OB2 ward at 7.20pm. Sister Callan, who was the most senior sister, Staff Nurse Ford and I got the ward report and then it was all go until the morning. This was going to be seven nights on and five nights off. Both Staff Nurse Ford and Sister Callan were wonderful people; I learned a lot from them. Whilst Staff Nurse Ford dealt with all the medicines, Sister Callan helped me change and feed the babies and give Ovaltine to the adults. We had most of the patients settled by midnight and then it was time to eat. So that was my job. I would put the soup on, peel the potatoes and put the chip pan on. Then I would chip the potatoes, set three trays and take Sister's soup upstairs to her office. We had our soup downstairs. Then, when the chips were ready, I would drop the three eggs into the chip pan, and they only took one minute to cook. They were lovely and fluffy. One night, Sister Callan took her torch and went out of the back door. I thought she must have heard a prowler but she came back with a bowl of strawberries from the garden in the hospital grounds. They were delicious.

Tuberculosis was at a very serious level in the Forties and Fifties, with many deaths. Sanatoriums were opened and most of the patients were nursed outside on verandahs: rest, fresh air and a good diet was the treatment. Then the research medical team decided to pump air into the pleural space, collapse the lung affected and rest it. It was a long stay for TB patients. The very ill ones were so thin and had to have their pressure areas treated. The others were coughing up horrible sputum about every half an hour, which meant renewing the sputum mugs regularly – not a nice job but it had to be done. Then: alleluia! Streptomycin was the new treatment in the early Fifties. So Sister Callan and I would sterilise all our glass syringes and needles – twenty-eight of them – draw up 2ml of sterile water, inject it into the bottles of streptomycin powder and shake it vigorously for two minutes. This was a time-consuming job. It was good to see them all ready for the morning. Then all the breakfast trays had to be laid in the kitchen for the patients and babies' feeds had to be made up for the morning. It was hard work being on nights. The first thing in the morning was the bedpan, bottle and potty round. Once that was over then it was the TB injections. There were a good number of patients; most of them would have their posteriors all exposed for me to save time! It was an injection that had to be given slowly otherwise it could be painful. A good massage soon dispersed it quickly. The patients christened me the "Jagger Queen". I quite liked the name.

We had a young girl who was eighteen years old, named Maureen. She had been in for one year and was very ill. She was becoming more emaciated as the weeks passed. We had to call the priest for last rites. Then the streptomycin arrived in 1952. We had to lift Maureen's skin to inject underneath, as she had no muscle at all. We had to massage it all away for five minutes. We just prayed that we would see a change in her. Well, we did – as we did with all the other TB patients. But, as time went on, the tubercle bacillus was becoming resistant to streptomycin, so then they had to find something else to weaken the bacillus so that the strept could do its job. So out came a cachet (the size of a £1 coin) with a powder enclosed in rice paper. The only way they could swallow it was by dipping it in water so that it would slide down the throat. If it burst, the patients were violently sick because of the taste. These cachets (PAS) were replaced by a small tablet called isoniazid. A doctor explained it in easy terms: this little tablet paralysed the bacillus so that the strept could attack. Well, as the months passed, Maureen was looking good.

We could see an improvement every day. She got her appetite back, put on weight and was looking pretty. She lived to marry and have children – thanks to strept. We had many wonderful recoveries. It was a turning point due to this miraculous drug.

Seven nights was an exhausting stretch of time because we came off duty in the morning, had breakfast and then went straight up to the lecture room for one hour at 9.00am. When the week was over it was a great feeling to know that I had five days off. I went home on Monday morning and slept for twenty-four hours. Tuesday I was ready to go into town to meet up with the rest of the nurses in Malloco's coffee shop. There were six of us: my room-mate Janet, Nan, Bridget, Isobel and Margaret. We would also meet with Jimmy and Gordon, as well as one set of cousins, both named Tom and two other friends, both called Bill. We would congregate at the coffee shop and then go to the cinema. We had four cinemas in Dunfermline town; today, there is only one. They were very nice chaps: gentlemen and with good personalities. We often went to the Glen, which is a beautiful place donated to the people by Andrew Carnegie. We would sing, recite poetry and tell funny jokes. I can't remember ever going into a pub with the boys. Young girls wouldn't dream of going into a pub in the Fifties. As mammy said to Scarlett O'Hara, "it just ain't fitting".

After my five nights off, I had to go back on Saturday and go to bed at 2.00pm and be on the ward for 7.20pm for another seven nights. In April 1952 we got a telephone call to inform us that the ambulance was on its way with a young male from my village with meningitis. Well, we knew this patient was in a bad way by the noise and obstreperous behaviour: movements due to the pressure of the fluid on the brain. In the ambulance was the driver, nurse, two policemen and the parents, all trying to keep Jimmy from hurting himself. We had the room all ready; Dr Martin was standing by with the lumbar puncture trolley all ready to drain the fluid off the brain via the lower spine. We had to keep the policemen to help keep Jimmy still; he was too strong for us to hold down. After Dr Martin measured the spinal fluid with a manometer he knew how much penicillin to inject into the lumbar space. Jimmy certainly settled down a bit and became less noisy, but we decided to lay out the mattress on the floor for the night until morning. He was in a coma for months and fed with a nasal tube. We timed his bodily functions so that we hardly ever had a wet bed, so there was no need for a catheter. It appeared that lumbar punctures were becoming less necessary, which was a good sign.

It was December and the decorations were going up. The Christmas tree was just outside the office and Jimmy's cubicle. Christmas Day arrived and I could hear all the nurses coming up the gangway with their red capes on, singing carols. I was washing Jimmy's face and attending to his oral hygiene when the nurses all marched in singing *Away in a Manger*. It sounded so lovely with an echo. I was just taking my gown off and washing my hands in the disinfectant when this voice said, "Merry Christmas, Jean." Well, at first I thought someone had come into the room but the door was still shut. I looked at Jimmy; he had his eyes open and he said it again.

"Oh! My goodness!" I said. "And a happy Christmas to you, Jimmy!" I almost cried, but instead I had to tell the choir of nurses in the corridor. What a great Christmas present! Jimmy could have two pillows now and was sitting up the next morning waiting for a little porridge. Now I would say that was a miracle. These are the wonderful memories that live with you for years after, especially considering he was a very ill man. Another man came in with acute pneumonia. When he came in we knew he was not going to make it. He was unconscious, so Janet came up from OBI ward to sit with him. He died in the morning, which meant that Staff Nurse Ford had to ring the police and they informed the parents or relatives. Houses in villages had no telephones in 1950. We had a telephone box at the bottom of our road and if I wanted a message to get to my parents I would ring that phone and whoever was passing answered it and delivered my message.

When the parents and the brother of the deceased came to the covered porch outside, Janet went to the door and fell back – she was not expecting to see the identical twin brother of the lad who had just passed away. Janet had to sit down with the relatives and have a cup of tea to recover in the porch. We had a special room at the mortuary where we laid the deceased and the relatives could visit their loved ones. I always dreaded taking the family down to that room. I always had tears in my eyes. When on night duty, if a patient died we had to ring the boiler man to come. We didn't have a porter. Jimmy Donald was a small-framed man. He reminded me of an unnerving film star, Peter Lorre, in the Fifties.

The mortuary was some distance from the wards and it was all downhill on a gravel path. So it wasn't easy pushing a heavy body on a slippery trolley. It was horrendous in the winter at night, going down a slippery slope on ice with snow, holding on to the deceased with "Peter Lorre", who was terrified. He had been at the hospital since it opened but he was still a nervous wreck carrying out that task. When I got back to the ward I then had to seal the room up for fumigating. We had a container on the floor in the middle of the cubicle with sulphur tablets that we set light to. The room would fill up with smoke for two to three hours. When the time was up, someone had to run in to open the window and would rush out with streaming eyes.

I was so glad when night duty was over. Now it was Scarlet Ward for me. I loved looking after children. The sister was Cathie Wallace from my village, who had spoken to me about nursing. We were not allowed to call one another by our first name – it was just our surname. Using the first name was looked on as being too familiar. Sister Wallace was very nice and ran very organised wards. There were sixteen beds in one ward and sixteen cots in the other. The cots were for boys and girls up to six years old. The beds were for the seven- to eleven-year-olds. Scarlet fever was only a childhood illness: a very high temperature (pyrexia), a sore throat, a white spotted, red tongue, a red rash and a white circle all round the mouth called "circum oral pallor" (COP). Scarlet fever was easy to diagnose with this. Most of the children had head lice so we had to deal with that straight away. On visiting days the parents would hand in little food parcels to Sister at the door, then look through the window to see their child. Tears were always shed – by children and parents. Children were kept in bed for one week and then got up and dressed in the second week. They were ready to go home (with a clean head of hair) at the beginning of the third week.

All the children wore white gowns tied down the back, as it was much easier when sitting them on the potty. When Matron paid her visit she would call out to the children, "Good morning, children!"

And they would all say together, "Good morning, Matron." I remember one little boy stood up in his cot, lifted his gown and curtsied. I saw a smile over Matron's face. Before the children had their meals they wore quite big bibs. (This saved a lot of laundry.) They had nice little trays with smaller crockery. In the second week of recovery, children got up to sit at the table; then they could go into the playroom after being washed and dressed.

One day we had two little four-year-old boys admitted – Billy and Benny. We put them in the cots near the kitchen window so that we could keep an eye on them whilst we were in the kitchen laying all the trays, making sandwiches for tea, peeling oranges and apples and slicing bananas. All the other meals came over from the main kitchen, but teatime was our responsibility.

Billy and Benny soon settled down after two days. Benny was a very quiet little boy. The only time he spoke was when he wanted a drink or the potty. Now Billy was the opposite: he was noisy, rattling the cot sides. He appeared like a little bully.

The fourth day we couldn't understand why little Benny's cot was always wet when we came to tidy it. He always used the potty. Then I asked the other nurses if Billy "the bully" had used the potty the same number of times as Benny but they said sometimes but not as often. So I decided to keep a closer eye on Billy, who never had a wet cot. As I was watching – lo and behold – I couldn't believe it. Billy climbed out of his cot, climbed into Benny's and did his business, the little rascal! Well, we soon put a stop to that little caper. The children loved teatime: their eyes used to light up when they saw their plates with their Marmite or fish paste sandwiches, a wedge of apple, two orange segments, a biscuit, two squares of chocolate, four smarties and two jelly babies. Oh, they wanted to gobble down the sweets first, but soon learned the discipline and rules in hospital. All the sandwiches had to be eaten first. Benny became more talkative and enjoyed playing with Billy in their second week, with no more wet cots. I did enjoy my spell on Scarlet Ward.

I was also enjoying meeting up with the gang at the coffee shop. Whilst I was on nights, Nan and Jimmy, Isobel and Bill, Bridget and Gordon as well as Janet and Bill had become close as couples. However, we still went around together. We had to write our name in a book if we wanted a late pass, which was for 11.30pm but with no more than two a week. The big doors would be locked at 8.30pm, which meant you had to dash down the gangway at 7.20pm, have a quick supper, rush upstairs, get dressed and get out quickly before the night sister locked the door. At the end of my second year, the painters were working on the outside of the building with big ladders. Well, Janet, Isobel and I were invited to a party and we had forgotten to put our names in the book by 9.00am for a late pass. So, when we went down for tea, we had a word with the painters and asked them to leave the ladder against my open window. "No problem," they said. So off we went to the party that evening. We were back at midnight. Janet started climbing first then Isobel. I started, got to the top and in a hushed voice said, "All right, girls?" lifting my leg into the room but the girls didn't answer me, so I said it again and then this voice said, "Come in, nurse."

Well, I nearly fell backwards because I recognised Matron's voice. Janet and Isobel were sitting on my bed trying hard not to laugh. Oh, yes, we were on the carpet in the morning. She gave us a lecture, then she said, "I will tell you this, nurses: no man will spoil the rose he means to wear."

When we came out of the office we were giggling and saying to one another, "What was that all about?" But, to be fair, we were all in her care and she was responsible for our welfare and safety.

Another time the matron made us jump was at one of our Sunday midnight feasts in the sitting room, in the dark, listening to Radio Luxembourg from 11.00pm to midnight. We should have all been in bed with the lights out at 11.00pm but we just couldn't miss our top twenty hits. This was 1952 and there were terrific singers and songs at that time. We were all tucking into the food when Rena said, "Shush! What was that?" Then we heard a creaky board. Slowly the door opened and this dark form stood in the doorway. Yes! It was Matron in her bell tent dressing gown and her frilly nightcap. She said, "Time you were in bed, nurses," and left. Luckily, the top twenty was finished so we didn't mind, but it didn't deter us from carrying on doing the same thing again. We took the risk but I think the matron was just letting us know that she was still in charge and that we were not to forget it.

We were all studying hard for our final exams in the third year. The lads were missing our company at the coffee shop. I allowed myself one night at the ballroom in the week but no cinema. Summer was over so we were all waiting for the dates of our exam days. September was the month and the letters arrived from the medical examining board in Edinburgh. Janet, Betty and I had the same date, which soon came round. That night,

Sister Callan was on her nights off, but she kindly said she would come with us as she knew where the examining halls were. We boarded the train at 9.00am and in going over the Forth Bridge we did the customary Scottish tradition – we threw a penny out of the window into the Firth of Forth for good luck. We arrived on time with lots of people milling around. Then we sat down to our written examination. It was a two-hour paper starting at 10.00am. Midday soon came round so we looked for Sister Callan and we all went to lunch.

Betty then asked me, "Oh what did you put down for that question about umbilicus?" I told her not to think about it and to enjoy her lunch. Then she told us she didn't know what they wanted so she just wrote that it was the "belly button". We didn't say anything. Poor Betty: I think they wanted more than that on the paper. After lunch all three of us started our practical at 1.00pm. We had samples of urine to test, with all the equipment needed, such as the urinometer, chemicals, Bunsen burners and a wooden grip for the test tubes. (Not like today, where one has a strip of paper with bands that change colour when dipped into the specimen.)

As I was doing my testing I looked across at some disturbance and Betty had flames coming from the wooden grip that she had on the test tube over the Bunsen burner. She had put the grip too low down the tube. Well, our practical was over. Then we had to go into another room, where six examiners were sitting at a long table. We sat down opposite the woman for our oral questions. When one had asked her questions, we moved onto another. They covered everything from hygiene to ventilation, from dietetics to diagnosing rashes and knowledge of the incubation periods of most diseases. I was glad when that session was over. It was now 4.00pm and we were starving. Sister Callan met us after she had done a bit of shopping and we all went to a nice tearoom. After getting the train back we had a good evening meal at the hospital and then went to bed at 9.00pm for a well-deserved sleep, ready for duty in the morning. We waited two weeks for our results. Janet and I passed but the farmer's daughter, Betty, failed her practical – but she passed on a resit. So we were now called staff nurses, with a little white bow under our chin and a diploma with the title "registered fever nurse". I was now capable of doing ambulance duty, which I had dreamed about doing when I was young.

My first case was to collect a child from a farmhouse off the main road. We went up this bumpy, potholed lane. It was a pitch-black night with not a light to be seen. At first I thought we had taken the wrong turn, then I saw a glimmer of light, so we kept going. The light got brighter so I got my torch and red blanket. The driver stopped and we expected to find the house but instead we ended up in a pigsty with a big sow feeding all her piglets. Then we heard the farmers call out to us, "Over here!"

The light in the house was from an oil lamp. My torch was very bright so I was able to see the child's throat and rash and make a diagnosis. We also took the particulars of name, date of birth, religion etc. So this was my first measles case.

The next day I was on the road to pick up another child in the neighbouring village and most of these villages were mining villages. The majority of miners had greyhounds. My father had one to catch rabbits for dinner, whereas others used them to race. Well, as I entered this house the child was in a chair and the two greyhounds were in bed with their heads on the pillows! I said to the parent that the child should be in the bed instead of the dogs and his answer was, "Oh, but they're running in the 2.30pm tomorrow." When I looked at the child I could see by the COP that he had scarlet fever.

Sometimes the driver and I would have a right chuckle at some of the answers we got back from the parents. Most of the houses had six to eight children and a few with ten. Birth control clinics only came about in the late 1960s. I remember asking a father the name of the ill child and he turned round to the wife and said, "Is that Willie or Tommy?" I think there were ten in that family. Another father stuck his chest out proudly when I asked what the religion of the child was and he said, "Oh, we are British."

One funny story that was told in our village was that a father was in charge of putting his children to bed and when his wife came home he told her that one child was crying and wouldn't settle so she went to investigate and found the child belonged to the family next door!

The most enjoyable time I had on ambulance duty was taking the children home when they were well. I would have two or three children in the posh black car all excited to see their parents, brothers and sisters. I did three months on ambulance duty and then I was ready to move on to do my general nursing. By this time, Nan had set a date to marry Jimmy, Janet was engaged to Bill and Isobel was engaged to another Bill. Rena and Bridget were going to do general nursing too but in the same town; I wanted to go further afield. I applied to the Royal Infirmary, Edinburgh, but they had a two-year waiting list. The next place available was on the outskirts of Edinburgh called Bangour General, near Bathgate. I was sorry to leave the fever hospital and all my friends, but we all promised to keep in touch and we did when they all got married and had their children. I was accepted at Bangour, but I spent one month at home with my mother and father. I had a few lovely days out with them and visited the ballroom and the coffee shop. Then it was time to pack my case again – a much bigger one this time – because I would only be home one weekend a month. My general training would only take two years because I had completed my fevers training, otherwise it would have been three years. My mother came to the train station to see me off. I told her I would write – which I did, twice a week. I enjoyed writing letters to all my friends.

Well, I arrived at Waverley Station, Edinburgh, and took the Bathgate bus, which took three to four hours. Princes Street was a very busy street. The bus stopped at the big hospital sign and I could see the minibus waiting to take all who got off down the winding road through a farm, past a mental health hospital and eventually arriving at the general hospital. This hospital had been a training camp for the army during the war, so it was isolated and spread out. The nurses' quarters were like prisoners' huts in the film *The Great Escape*. The minibus ran every twenty minutes to the main road and the last pick-up was at 11.00pm; it was a ten- to fifteen-minute journey. It was horrendous and frightening if you missed the last minibus because the mental health hospital was a forbidding place. The windows only opened three inches at the bottom but the patients would be shouting with disturbing noises. I would run like blazes all the way back.

On site we had two male wards (surgical and medical), two female wards (surgical and medical), a children's ward, a maternity ward, a gynaecology ward, a plastic unit, a TB ward, two theatres, a large dining room and a recreation hall. Matron had her house next to the consultant surgeon, Mr Milnes, then there were the doctors' quarters. The sisters' quarters were next to the doctors'. It was quite a large area, all spread out. Our rooms were lovely: good beds, nice dressing table and wardrobe. We also had central heating because it was a cold, desolate spot where the winds were strong. So I was very pleased with my chosen hospital to train for two years, We could wear our uniforms outside but had to wear our coat, pillbox hat, black stockings and black rubber-soled shoes.

The lecture room was next to the recreation hut. We all introduced ourselves – six girls and one man: eight, including me – on the Monday morning. The tutor, Miss Baker, informed us which wards we would be working in and also the days and times of our lectures. The lectures would be given by medical and surgical registrars; the practical sessions were led by the tutor. The one man in our group was a Jim McKadie. He was about six feet two inches tall, slim and aged approximately forty. It seemed strange to us that he was starting his general training at such a late stage, but then he told us he had been a mental health nurse for twenty-two years. It turned out that Jim was very clever and also had a photographic mind; he was also very comical. I thought he should have been on the stage. He reminded me very much of Jerry Lewis, the film star. He made everybody laugh so much. He didn't write any lectures down so the doctors thought he was wasting time. Then they would ask Jim to take over and sure enough he would give us the anatomy and functions of any organ we were discussing. Even the doctors were amazed.

All the sisters in the wards were between thirty and forty years of age, very dedicated, very kind but very strict. The wards were spotless – neat and well organised. Sister Chisolm was on the male medical ward. She was my favourite – very smart in appearance and loved her ward. Even on her day off she would come over and look in the door just to make sure the ward was running smoothly. When patients were to be admitted she was there to inspect them. If they came from a "down and out" centre known as "a doss house" she would turn to the nurse and say, "Get that man in the bath." She was always right because they would be lousy. One day she looked at another admission on the trolley, turned to the driver and said, "Get that man in the mortuary."

She was very particular about her beds: the patients who were very ill and unkempt also had a bed bath straight away and all the beds had blue top covers with pink tulips. She would stand at the door in the morning, look down the thirty-bedded ward and spot a cover that was the wrong way round, with the tulips facing down. It had to be changed immediately. She also made sure that every nurse knew every detail of all thirty patients: name, age, religion, illness and medication. When the dinner trolley was wheeled in, we all stood in a line with our trays. Sister dished up the food herself, arranging everything beautifully on the plate and wiping off any smudges of gravy from the edge. The special diets for a few patients she prepared herself in our own small kitchen. We went through the same routine for supper. For breakfast, the night nurse would put two trays with thirty sausages each in a slow oven. We had two big frying pans and Sister would put her cook apron on, use the fat from the sausages and fry triangular pieces of bread. Other mornings it would be boiled or scrambled eggs.

The patients loved their meals. The sausages were the best. If there were any leftovers, Sister would make little sandwiches for the patients' tea at 3.00pm. Of course they also had coffee or tea with a biscuit at 11.00am. Sister Chisolm always said, "Feed them well and with medication you get a quick recovery." She also had a brandy bottle. She allowed the night nurse to give the old boys with urinary problems a nip of brandy or a drop of Guinness. It always worked wonders: they would sleep all night. Sister always looked on her patients as family and never forgot to tell all the new nurses to do the same. She was so kind-hearted and I remember one particular elderly man from the "doss house" with very dirty torn clothes. We undressed him in the bathroom, where the fleas were jumping, and we managed to get him in the bath. His clothes all went in the bin. Once he had a good wash he felt much better and his breathing was much improved. He said, "I think that's what I needed."

He had just fallen on hard times. He was with us a week and with the good food he looked well. Sister went to the cupboards and kitted the old boy out with underclothes, jacket, trousers, jumper and socks. She appealed to the Women's Institute and various charities for men's clothing. I enjoyed working on her ward and learned a lot about medicine.

I was transferred to the male surgical ward. Again, it was spotless, but looked a lot busier, with lots of drip stands and wooden frames with pulleys attached to a few beds. The mix of patients were elderly, with broken hips or prostatectomies, and young men with compound fractures of the femur or shattered bones in the legs due to motorbike or work accidents. They were usually long-stay. The leg would be put in a sling in the wooden frame and the pulley would have weights on the bottom, pulling the bone to realign the break into the right position. The weights were added gradually every week, which meant the patient could be in bed for two months. During the hot weather the patient would ask for the window to be opened above his bed; they were tall windows that only opened down at the top, so the nurse would step on a chair, then onto the side locker and pull the window down. Of course, when she looked down all she saw was a sea of faces beaming up at her. It was a view no man could resist, black stockings and suspenders. I think every nurse in the ward opened a window knowing she made some patients feel good. It was better having happy men than grumpy ones.

I remember the day Mr Henry came in as a road accident. Seemingly he had stopped his car to go to the aid of another accident victim, who wasn't badly hurt, when another car smashed into him. He was forty-five years old and his spine was shattered in quite a few places. He was laid on a stabilising frame attached to the bed, face-down, with two bolts on either side of his head and a long rod to keep the spine in place. The poor man was in that position for three months – it was very awkward when doing his bodily functions the wrong way up. Mr Henry was a proper gentleman. I always washed him thoroughly when he had used the bedpan. It took a good fifteen to twenty minutes to wash all his private parts and of course sometimes he would get an erection and he was so apologetic. I would tell him not to worry about it because it didn't bother me. I did feel sorry for him. One day I came on duty at 1.00pm and Mr Henry called for me, very upset. The nurse had not washed him properly and visiting time was 2.00pm. So I got my bowl of water and made him all fresh and clean again but it took me a lot longer than fifteen minutes. I was furious and went to confront the nurse responsible. I said, "Don't you dare leave Mr Henry in a state like that again!" I went on, "Just think of your father in Mr Henry's place for three months and give him the care that you would give your father." After my lecture she apologised to Mr Henry.

When the three months were up Mr Henry was rotated on the frame so that he was looking at the ceiling in a normal position. It was much easier for him in every way. He was to lie in this position for another three months. I was then to do night duty on this ward. Fortunately I had Jim McKadie, who was a relief nurse, helping out on all the wards where he was needed. A staff nurse was always on a ward. Jim was a morale booster. He was like a grown-up kid and created funny situations on the ward. One of the night sisters was ready for retirement and she would shuffle round the wards doing her rounds. She would bend over every patient and say, "Good morning, and how are you?"

And the patient might say, "Oh, feeling better," or, "not so well."

She would then say to every patient, "Good, that's fine."

So McKadie would jump into an empty bed, draw the covers up to his chin and wait for her to ask how he was. He would say in a frail voice, "I feel very weak and my life is ebbing away."

She then would say "Good, that's fine."

After she left, McKadie would jump out of bed and would run down to the women's ward, put a white cap on his head and do exactly the same. He certainly entertained all of us on night duty.

Well, Mr Henry was now off the frame and having physio on the bed every day. He made great progress and I said goodbye to him as he walked out on crutches with his wife.

When on nights, our meal was at midnight. One nurse from each ward would make their way to the canteen, which was a good 200 yards down the road. In the winter it was freezing, so we would all meet up wrapped in blankets and McKadie looked like a washerwoman with a shawl round his head. I remember one night the snow was three inches deep and we had a snowball fight. Another time, McKadie lifted up tiny Mary Simpson onto his shoulders and ran down the road with her – and she was yelling her head off. We were all ready for a lovely three-course meal when we reached the canteen. The food was first-class. The home sister, who lived in the nurses' quarters, was a lovely person. She was around fifty years old, short, buxom and motherly. She had two beautiful Persian cats named Princess and Duchess. These cats were like her children: they slept in dolls' cots with pillows and blankets. They would always sit outside Sister's office.

Sister Green did her job really well, looking after all the nurses – especially the young ones just starting their training. There were no restrictions about coming and going; we all had our own keys, not like the fever hospital. The sister had a book in her office where you wrote in your day off, and on that day the maid would bring a lovely tray with tray cloth, small teapot, water and milk jug and a miniature vase with flowers. Breakfast would include bacon, eggs, tomatoes, fried bread, toast and marmalade. Sister laid the trays herself and also looked after the nurses who had the flu or any other ailment. We also had a staff sick bay for more serious cases.

One day McKadie wheeled the big laundry basket and put Princess and Duchess in it and of course the van came and collected the basket and took it away to the main laundry building. She was calling them and then realised they could have been stolen. They were beautiful cats. A notice went up on the noticeboard offering a reward of £10 for the whereabouts of her cats. So McKadie went and collected them and received the reward. She gave him a kiss on the cheek and McKadie bent down and said to the cats, "Now don't wander off again!" He even said it like Jerry Lewis, pointing his finger at the cats.

The next day, he put tiny Mary Simpson in the basket. Of course, once the lid is closed, it cannot be opened without a key. The workers came to collect the laundry, heard her call "help" and set her free.

They were a grand lot of nurses. We all learned to play badminton and became so good we played other clubs from the surrounding areas. We all did our shopping in Edinburgh and Bathgate. We wore our uniforms because the conductors or conductresses would pass us by when taking the fares. We also got into the cinema free of charge and received discounts in all the big stores in Edinburgh and Bathgate. We had a lot of respect in the 1950s from the public. The discount eventually spread out to the smaller shops. I would even have received a discount at the hairdressers if I had frequented it – but I didn't. I still cut my own hair.

All the hospitals in the UK had wonderful Christmas dinners for patients, staff and domestics. A few doctors would dress as Santa and with a sack on their backs would go round the wards and give presents to all of the patients. Then they would put a maid's apron and hat on to serve the dinners. Everybody contributed to make it all run smoothly. The wards were beautifully decorated and the tree stunning. It was hard work, but done for the patients' benefit. Being large wards the patients were like one big happy family. We did have side wards for the very ill patients. The visitors were allowed to stay longer on Christmas Day, Boxing Day and New Year's Day.

When Christmas was over we would have our Christmas dinner in the canteen, served by kitchen staff, and the week after we would serve the domestics and kitchen staff. The matron, sisters and doctors had their meal on a separate day all together. Everything was delightful, the tables beautifully laid with crackers, paper plates and delicious food. It was well organised because there were lots of sittings on the day. Another well-organised event was our annual hospital ball. All hospitals had one (the fever hospital held its ball in the Dunfermline Glen). The Bangour Hospital event was held in the hall just next to the kitchens. The invitations went out to the Bathgate Police and to an airport near Edinburgh. It was evening dress and black-tie affair with a good band and good food. It was strange seeing all the doctors dressed so smartly and with their dicky bows instead of their white coats.

The resident consultant surgeon lived in a nice house next to Matron's house. He was married with four children. He was approximately forty years of age. He was a jovial, good-looking man with charm, and he kept fit. He was a very good dancer and danced with Matron, the sisters and most of the nurses.

He would do his rounds in the morning after playing tennis dressed in his white shorts, carrying his racket and wearing white socks on brown legs. When he got to the women's ward they would all be excited. Most of the women had had their operations or were newcomers waiting to have theirs, but if they were overweight Mr Milne would put them on a diet until they were discharged. They were all waiting for his praise if they had lost weight. But some women deliberately got their visitors to bring in goodies and he would take them all away. Oh! They loved all the attention he gave them. However, when I went to do my spell in theatre for six weeks, I saw another side of Mr Milne. He was very impatient and had a temper.

We had windows in our theatre, though they were never opened. But many a time an instrument would be thrown over Mr Milne's shoulder and straight through the window. The carpenter would come immediately to block up the window. The first time I was in charge of the swab count at an operation he asked me for a swab count before stitching up the wound. I told him I was one swab short and he would shout, "Are you sure?"

And I would shout back "Yes sir, I'm sure."

Then he would lift his white boot, where he had deliberately stamped on a swab. He did this with all new staff, just to test

30

them out. I used the big swab forceps to take the swab off his boot and he would say, "Good girl."

He was a brilliant surgeon and lecturer. He would tell us all about the organ he was operating on, and then he would ask questions. I very much enjoyed theatre work, but it was much more enjoyable when McKadie came to join us.

We did all our cleaning at the weekend – both theatres and wards. The work was endless. Mr Milne looked into the theatre one Saturday morning asking for the Monday's list and he said, "Gosh, it's like a morgue in here!" So off he went and came back with a nice little radio for us: what a kind gesture! On Saturday morning we washed the walls and windows in the two theatres and cleaned two operating tables, the glass cabinets and sterilisers, anaesthetic machines, operating lights and floor. Sunday was spent making swabs and packing them in a drum, packing dressing towels into bigger drums, cleaning and oiling instruments, testing and repairing rubber gloves with a bicycle kit and packing them into a linen sachet cover separating left and right. Surgical needles were inspected for blunt ones. Different sizes and types – straight and curved – were arranged in their glass dishes, with strong surgical spirit poured over. Then all the drums went into the autoclave. The instruments were boiled up in the big sterilisers before operations. It was the same routine every weekend. I can honestly say we never had any infections in our wards: none whatsoever.

Well, my theatre time finished and I was sent to the female medical ward. Sister Grey was in charge. She was tall, slim and quiet but like all the other sisters kept a beady eye on the running of her ward.

Going to a new ward one had to learn everything about the patients: illnesses, medications, diets, names, ages and religions. Sister would call us into the office for the report on all the patients after breakfast.

I noticed on the ward a young girl called Helen who was

fourteen years old – very delicate-looking and pale. The sister then came out with Helen's diagnosis; I felt like I had been hit by a bombshell on hearing that she had leukaemia and had six weeks to live. Helen was allowed visitors at any time during the day rather than two hours in the afternoon and two hours in the evening. But I had decided to spend as much time with Helen as I could after my evening meal. I would finish at 7.30pm, have my meal and go back to keep Helen company. I would draw the screens round, put on the little lamp and it would be a jigsaw or a game of snap. Sometimes it would be a manicure or pedicure. I would leave around 10.00pm. She was too weak for all the manoeuvres of a bath so when her hair needed washing I took the headrail completely off the bed, lay Helen flat and drew the mattress up to the top, where I had a bowl of hot water. Supporting Helen's head, the hairdresser's set-up worked really well. Helen would laugh, as we had a few funny moments when things didn't turn out how they should have done. I would try a new hairstyle on Helen with curlers and wavers and we would end up laughing our heads off. However, I could see she was getting much weaker as the weeks went by, so out came the storybooks. Seemingly Helen had never been told that she was going to die, but she knew, because one night she just came out with it: "I'm going to die, aren't I, Nurse Shaw?" and I was so taken aback.

I said, "Yes, we all have to die, Helen. God must be very short of angels."

Then she said, "Will you be here?"

And I said, "You bet, Helen."

And she just said, "Good."

She was so brave and lovely. The doctors were not wrong about the time. I said goodnight to Helen; she was much weaker and breathless. Her parents had been sent for and I knew, when I climbed into bed that night, that Helen would not be there in the morning. I didn't want to believe it, but it was true. I was staring at an empty bed in the morning. I could not control my tears over the lovely girl who didn't get the chance to blossom into a young lady. I had a lot of heartache when I became friendly with patients and they lost the fight to live, but their memories linger on just like family members.

The cleaning programme on the wards was as thorough as that performed in the theatres; all wards were cleaned every morning at 9.00am. The patients loved it. We damp-dusted the screens, window ledges, bedside lockers, chairs and the back frames of the beds. On Saturdays, we wheeled the beds over to the left whilst the domestic mopped the floor with a mop bucket. We put the beds back and did the same with the right side. It was like a keep-fit class every week with *Housewives' Choice* on the radio, playing out all the lovely tunes. One Saturday per month, the floor had to be polished, so when we had all the beds wheeled over to one side one nurse would dollop a drop of red polish on the floor with a spatula. The domestics would rub it all in with a mop and then out would come the bumpers. We had two – and they could not be lifted – not even by a man. They were big, heavy metal oblong masses covered in felt on a long thick pole, but once you got them swinging from side to side it became easier – especially when we did it to music. It was fun and kept us fit. The men loved Saturday mornings looking at all the nurses' bodies swinging from side to side!

This cleaning routine kept down infection. The patients' water jugs and glasses were washed every morning, with nice little beaded covers over the jugs. The bed linen was changed every two days. The tulips were all wrapped in newspapers at night and stored in a bucket along with all the other flowers. Then, after all the cleaning was finished in the morning, the flowers would be arranged with the tulips all standing straight up and placed on the two large cabinets in the middle of the ward. The wards did look lovely. We always finished our cleaning chores by 11.00am, just in time for patients' and staff refreshments.

I don't think the nurses today would believe what we did in the 1950s. They would be dumbstruck. We all had brilliant training in the wards, at the patients' bedsides, but we were also caring about them keeping their dignity, brushing their hair and teeth, cutting their finger- and toenails and bed bathing them. I became a barber nurse and shaved the ill and elderly men. We worked forty-eight hours a week, with little pay, so a lot of trained nurses went out in droves to America for a lot more dollars.

My two-year general training was coming to an end, but before my exams I had to do my six weeks' duty on the children's ward. This ward was run by Sister Purvis, with twenty-six beds, which were always full. The small children's theatre was very close to the ward where the tonsillectomy and adenoidectomies (known as T&As) were performed. It was like an assembly line on Mondays and Thursdays on operating days. The children would be given a little sedative beforehand, wheeled up to theatre and given a little more anaesthetic, and the operation was done in fifteen minutes. They were wheeled back on their side, like limp little rabbits, coughing and spluttering. The first swallow of medication was always the worst, so I always made sure they got their medication before the pain started, and then you had a sleeping child. The next day they could have two to three spoonfuls of jelly. I was always cross with the nurses who were too late giving children their medication. It is a very painful operation and I am so pleased the numbers were drastically cut. The children were kept in for ten days.

Sister Purvis was short, of medium build and very kind. She made the most wonderful coffee at 11.00am every morning for the theatre staff, doctors and her own staff. She banned everyone from the kitchen until the coffee was ready. Margaret the domestic was the only one who knew how she made it, because Margaret made it when Sister had her days off. She put about a gallon of water in a huge pot with two teaspoons of salt, then the coffee, and brought it up slowly to boiling point. She would turn it off and let it stand for ten minutes, strain it through muslin with a ladle and – hey presto! – lovely coffee! Sister Purvis was good friends with Sister Chisolm and when they were going down the road together they walked and looked like Laurel and Hardy from the cinema. It was very comical when walking behind them.

It was now nearing the end of my two years' training and our exams were due. Luckily we didn't have to travel; they were held in our lecture room. It was much easier, as we knew where all the equipment was stocked on the shelves. The examiners came to us this time.

We all passed our exam so now I was a state registered nurse and a registered fever nurse. My two close friends, Grace Riddle, Cathie Watt and I had written to a maternity hospital in Camberwell, London, for a post to do midwifery and we were accepted.

My mother and neighbour came to the big occasion of being presented with our hospital badge and certificate. It was a beautiful day. The hall was laid out with a very nice buffet and drinks. I introduced Grace and Cathie to my mother and Mrs Jack, and then I showed them the wards and the nurses' home. We all had a wonderful day. I was looking forward to spending some time at home with my parents and meeting up with all my nurse friends from the fever hospital. Nan and Jimmy were married with two children; Isobel and Bill were married with one child; Bridget and Gordon had two children; and Rena and Ronnie were married (with me a bridesmaid) and with one child. I was sorry to leave Bangour so there were quite a few tears, but I knew I had to move on and I wanted to see the bright lights of London.

It was August 1957 and it was time to pack and leave home again. I said goodbye to my dad and brothers. My mother had decided to come into Edinburgh with me, so we got the train into Waverley Station. Grace and Cathie were there, waiting to meet me. We boarded the Flying Scotsman to King's Cross. Mum was standing at the window of the carriage and I could see she was tearful – as I was. I told her not to worry, that Grace, Cathie and I would look after one another and I would write every week. It was a very hot day when we arrived at King's Cross. We had to find the Underground trains and our cases were getting heavier and heavier. There was no wheeled luggage in those days. The Tube trains were stifling and hot. We had to get on three different trains and, because it was rush hour, stand all the way to the Oval. It felt good to be free of the Underground.

Now we had to ask directions to St Giles' Maternity Hospital and start walking. A taxi was out of the question; they were too expensive for us. At last we arrived, hot, thirsty and with an aching back and sore feet. We entered the front entrance, rang a bell, waited, waited and waited, until eventually a domestic came along. We gave our names. She went into the office and came out with three keys, told us where to go – and off she went. We climbed the stairs with our cases and it felt like climbing Everest. I took the first room, Cathie took the one next to me and Grace took the one just round the corner. When I saw my room I was shocked, I could not believe the state it was in. The room had a horrible smell, the washbasin was full of water and cigarette ends and the top bed cover was all stained. I was so angry because they had had two months' notice of our arrival. I went to see Cathie and Grace and they were not pleased with the cleanliness of their room either. We all three went downstairs to find the home sister – if there was one. But instead we found the domestic supervisor and complained to her.

She apologised to us and said they were very short of domestics but if we would like to go down for supper she would see to our rooms. Down we went to the dining room, where it was all self-service. We were starving, but the food was disappointing and on the chilly side. When we went back to our rooms the supervisor had made them more respectable. I unpacked my case and then sat down to write a few lines to my mother. It would have been nice to have picked up a phone and told her we had arrived safely.

Next morning we had to go to the linen room for our uniforms, but breakfast was first and it was pretty good and hot. It wasn't a friendly atmosphere in the dining room, so we made our way to the linen room, where we were handed two white coats and two caps. When I got dressed, I looked more like a supermarket shelf stacker or a bacon slicer in a grocery shop. They seemed to be short of everything here: no domestics, no waitresses, no proper uniforms, no friendly voices. Oh dear – not a good start! Grace, Cathie and I went to the same ward, which had thirty beds. We were introduced to the two sisters. One was quiet, the other one loud. We were taken round the ward, nursery, four labour rooms, the sluice and the kitchen, which had a huge fridge where all the bottles of expressed milk were stored to feed the babies during the night. The babies were only wheeled out during the day to the mothers at feed times then wheeled back to the nursery. All the mothers slept well at night, confined to bed for one week and in the second week going into the nursery, learning how to handle their babies – then home.

Grace, Cathie and I went to our first lecture and met another three nurses. Then we met the doctor. He knew we were Scottish so he tried to tell us a Scottish joke relating to labour. It rather backfired on him because he just didn't have the comical spark like a Scotsman. The start of our training was all done on the ward. We had to witness eleven births before we were allowed to deliver on our own. When I witnessed my first birth I just thought it was the most miraculous experience I had ever seen. I could not believe that this purple, limp little being was going to turn into this red, robust little baby getting more beautiful by the minute. So, I had witnessed my first birth and looked forward to the rest.

Cathie, Grace and I went to the Streatham Locarno. It was quite a large dance hall with a good band. We went there for Christmas and brought the new year in. We all came to the conclusion that we did not like St Giles' Hospital. The dining room left a lot to be desired. When we had a late supper, the mice would scuttle out for their supper. However, we said we would try and forget all the bad things about the place and be positive. It was difficult getting to witness all eleven births. I was either at lunch, at supper or off duty. It was now the end of 1958 and I needed to see one more birth and then I would be in the running to deliver my first baby. I didn't have to wait long. A young unmarried girl walked in off the street. She looked like she needed a good hot bath; however, she was in labour, so that was out of the question. The loud, bossy sister was in attendance. The girl became abusive and would not cooperate, shouting, "I don't want the little brat!"

The sister whacked her across the buttock and said, "Get pushing!"

After delivery the girl did not want to see the child; all she did was sign it up for adoption. She still had the mark on her buttock long after baby was born. Marching orders would have been in order for "Bossyboots" today. I was glad I had witnessed all my deliveries. But, as it was my birthday, I was looking forward to celebrating it with Cathie and Grace at the Locarno. The three of us were off duty at 4.30pm.

I was ready to follow Grace and Cathie out of the door when my exit was blocked by a big, Jamaican woman in labour, wailing and wiping her face. She looked very distressed. I was heading for the door when Sister "Bossyboots" shouted, "OK, nurse: she is your first delivery."

I said, "Oh, but, Sister, I have a 4.30pm."

And her reply was, "Oh no, my girl – off duty doesn't come in to it when you have to get your deliveries done."

Well, I knew we had to deliver twelve babies – but not in our time off. However, orders were obeyed without any backchat in those days. I had been accosted and I just had to control my feelings. A poor woman needed my assistance. In the 1950s all women in labour were given enemas. So a quick enema was administered, which really made things happen.

Teatime and suppertime came and went, but there was none for me. I had to stay and deliver this baby with the night sister in attendance. It was now 8.30pm; it was quite a struggle for this poor woman, but she soon delivered a baby boy weighing eleven pounds eight ounces – all that was missing was his boxing gloves. The mother did really well, with no complications. The time was 9.00pm.

The night sister said to me, "Well done!" and then she left.

I was glad it was all over. Now I had to make the mother comfortable and give her a cup of tea in a nice clean bed. I then had to attend to the baby: dress his umbilicus, measure and weigh him, place a name tag on his wrist, give him a light sponge over, wrap him up and take him to his mother. I wrote my report before rinsing all the sheets from the labour ward bed and putting them in a laundry bag. It was 11.30pm so I could go off duty. "Thank you very much!" I didn't feel hungry anymore, only feelings of anger.

When I got to my room, I was a bit tearful. Cathie and Grace had just come in and they couldn't believe that I had just come off duty. Then I told them I was leaving and handing in my notice the following morning. Cathie and Grace then said, "Well, if you are leaving – so are we!"

So we wrote our letters of resignation, ready to be handed in to Matron the next morning. We entered Matron's office, told her we were leaving, put our envelopes on the table and she immediately said, "Night duty tonight, for you three girls."

We felt like walking out, packing our bags and leaving right there and then but we knew that we had to keep to our contract and work two weeks' notice. Most of the work on night duty was spent in the nursery changing and feeding the babies. Grace was on the first floor, I was on the second and Cathie on the third. Grace and I managed to keep all babies contented and quiet but that wasn't the case with Cathie's lot. One night Grace came up the back stairs to see me and we decided to pop up the stairs to see Cathie for a minute. Well, we both burst out laughing. There was Cathie, sitting down with a baby over each shoulder trying to rock them. When she saw us she screwed her red face up and said, "I'm sick of this!"

She looked like the old woman who lived in a shoe, who had so many babies she didn't know what to do. Poor Cathie. We just had to leave her to it. The two weeks passed quickly and at last we were packing our cases and ready to leave. But, because we were known in the hospital as "the three musketeers," we felt like doing something that was not allowed and that was to walk and lie on the grass. We all had to sit on the benches. It was a nice warm day, so we lay on the grass and then we cooled our feet in the fish pond, right in front of Matron's office. She opened her window and shouted hysterically, "Get out, get out!"

Oh, we did feel good and no dead fish! It was a good feeling going out of the gate and going home. Well, we thought we were going back up to Scotland when Grace said "Hey, girls, why don't we try private nursing?" So we went into the phone box and looked up private nursing agencies in the directory. We rang Miss Hill's secretary and were accepted over the phone. Grace was given the address of an elderly gentleman in Finchley who wanted a live-in nurse. I was given a vacancy in an orphanage in Harlesden – Cathie was to go to a nursing home in Brighton.

First we had to make our way to the agency at Archway in the dreaded Tube, to give all our particulars and sign a contract. Miss Hill was a very pleasant lady. She told us where we could buy our white uniforms made of poplin. This was a lovely soft material that washed like a dream – no ironing needed. White shoes were to be worn. We also had to purchase an expense

Martha and James Shaw (my mother and father) in Dunfermline Glen.

Me and Rena Duncan with the Fever Hospital behind us.
Later, I was a bridesmaid at Rena's wedding.

This was taken at Inverforth House.
It was opened by the Queen Mother in 1961.

On the steps of Inverforth House with the Union members' wives who were 'recruited' as patients for the hospital opening - despite being physically well.

On my lunch break at Greenways Nursing Home.

Christmas 1952, with my dear roommate Janet, who is sadly no longer with us.

This was the OBI ward with Sister Horsborough (front) in the dark uniform. I am on the left with Staff Nurse Archibald on the right. (Back row) Christie the domestic, Janet, Margaret(domestic), Nicky and Nancy with all our tiny patients.

and receipt book, which meant that we were responsible for presenting our bill to the patient with travelling expenses and extra hours added. The patient had to provide two meals daily and two on night duty. Granted, the wages were more than with the NHS but it was a twelve-hour shift and no paid holidays. We would also be responsible for keeping up with tax payments. We soon got everything settled with the agency, made our way to the Tube station and worked out which lines we each wanted to take. We said our goodbyes and promised to write. This was to be the end of a beautiful friendship that had lasted three years.

Well, I arrived at the orphanage at around 7.00pm. The matron welcomed me with a cup of tea, toast, cheese and a lovely piece of cake. She then introduced me to Judy, the other nurse, who was the same age as me. I was expecting more staff but that was it, just the three of us, with two daily domestics to do the cleaning, washing and ironing. The matron did all the cooking; she was a very good cook and a super baker. The children were all asleep, so I was taken up to my room and it was very comfortable. I slept very well after a hectic day. I got up the next morning at 7.00am, then Judy took me in to meet the children. The eldest was six years old and the youngest fifteen months. There were fourteen children: nine boys and five girls. Two boys had cerebral palsy (known then as spastic), but Matron took care of them. I just had to get them ready for breakfast for 9.00am. We had two square, low tables and chairs and four high chairs for the babies. After feeding the babies, Judy sat at one table and I was at the other with my knees up to my chin (because of the height of the table). It was so uncomfortable, but it was only for half an hour.

The children were very quiet and well behaved at the table. Matron would feed the two boys with cerebral palsy. If it was a nice day she would carry them into the garden and lie them in a blanket under a big umbrella. Judy and I put the children's coats and shoes on them for their morning walk. We had two big black twins' prams. I put my two youngest inside, top and bottom, with two holding on at either side of the hood and two either side of the handle. Judy had the same, so off we went in different directions with our six children for a two-and-a-half-hour walk. The children were a delight to take out; they would never let go of the pram for a second. They just trotted with me in a very quiet manner. I thought these children were orphans, but not all of them. Judy then told me that most of them had been abused. So, when the parents came to visit, they were never left alone with their child. Sometimes I wished that the parents would not be allowed to visit because the children ended up crying when they left. Rainy days were not good. We had to play games indoors instead of the nice garden, although they did have an hour's nap at 2.00pm.

I had been at the orphanage for six months and I had the feeling I had to move on. I was drawn back to the NHS but first I had to apply for a job and inform the agency. Fortunately, Judy lived in a two single-bedded room just about fifteen minutes' walking distance and said I could move in with her until I got a post in an NHS hospital. Meanwhile, the agency was replacing me. The next morning, I happened to look out of the window and there was the black pram and children going past and I couldn't believe who was with them – only Grace!

I opened the window and shouted, "Don't lose any, now!"

Grace looked up dumbstruck. She brought the children in, we had a cup of tea and she gave me all the news, telling me that Cathie had gone back home. It was good to see Grace again. She had a flat in Finchley so I got her phone number and we said our goodbyes.

Grace didn't stay long at the orphanage. I didn't think she would, somehow. I decided to ring Willesden General Hospital, which was nearby, instead of writing. I spoke to the matron on the Friday and she said that there was only one vacancy in the theatre: would I be interested? I said yes but that I hadn't done theatre work for two years. She didn't think that that would be a problem and I could move in the following day, starting on the Monday, in September 1958. It was a small cottage hospital. The rooms were very pleasant and the staff very friendly. The theatre was small, the sister in charge was between thirty and forty years old, with lots of make-up on and quite vain. She was the type to look in the mirror when she spoke to you. I had only been there two days when I met the consultant surgeon. He was six feet in height with a red crew cut and stark naked, with his hand covering his private parts, asking me for a bar of soap for the shower. Sister soon put him in his place. She told me he was a lovely, pleasant man, harmless and a bit of a tease – especially with new staff – wondering what their reaction would be. His actions brought back memories of the surgeon in Scotland hiding the swabs under his boot. But this one was hiding the soap in the shower.

I made new friends, two Irish girls, Annie and Rose, and Maureen, who was very well spoken with a quiet manner. They introduced me to the Hammersmith Palais, where Joe Loss was the resident band. It was a terrific band with three good singers. Joe Loss was the bandleader – full of energy. I loved the music and the hall was always packed. I am so fortunate to have experienced dancing to his music before he left for fame and fortune on TV and playing on the *Queen Mary* liner.

I had been at the hospital for three months when Maureen asked me to go to the Palais with her that night; I had been the night before and didn't really want to go, but she pleaded with me. I relented and went with her. Well I have Maureen to thank because that was the night I met my husband Robert.

Theatre work I enjoyed. I had to do two "on calls" for emergencies as well as every other weekend, which meant I had to stay on the premises. However, one nurse left, which increased my "on calls". I wasn't very happy about that – being cooped up in the hospital. I was missing my boyfriend, the Palais and the cinema. Then, to crown it all, the sister's mother became ill so she had to take compassionate leave, which left me in charge, doing even more "on calls". I felt so imprisoned that I went to Matron to hand in my letter of resignation. I worked my two weeks' notice; the sister was back and I was a free agent.

It was now May 1959. I had to find a place to live and ring up the private agency and speak to Miss Hill. The newsagents had lots of room vacancies on their board. So I picked one out in Willesden Green. The house was near the Tube station – which was good. The lady of the house was Mrs Jacobs, who lived on her own. The room was clean, with a small gas ring on the tiled fireplace – not ideal, but I could always boil an egg for breakfast. So I decided to stop here until I found somewhere better. Mrs Jacobs was a thrifty little lady. There was no shower and I had to tell her when I wanted a bath because she controlled the heating of the water in her kitchen. I was then told that I could only have four inches of water. Not only that, but I could only have two baths a week.

I kept scanning the newsagent's room vacancy cards and then I saw one about 200 yards up the road from Mrs Jacobs. I went straight away to see the room. Mrs Leberman was another Jewess – very friendly and motherly, I liked her straight away. She was married to George, who was just as nice. When I saw the room I said, "Oh yes, this is fine."

Firstly, there was no smell of gas; there was a nice little Belling cooker with a small oven in the corner, and it was cheaper. I went down to tell Mrs Jacobs I would be moving out the next day and she was none too happy. I was now in a cosy room with a bathroom and plenty of hot water. I could do my own washing and hang it out in the garden.

Mrs Leberman was seventy years of age and George was eighty. After being there a few weeks I would help George in the garden and cut the lawn. Mrs Leberman would call up to me to come and get slices of cake she had baked and a bowl of her chicken noodle soup, which was delicious. They were a lovely couple. It was a big house with four large rooms and my single one. Mrs Leberman and George had their bedroom downstairs. I got to know two Irish private nurses, Mary and Bridget, who rented one room. Being St Patrick's Day, they invited me along to the Galtymore dance hall in Cricklewood. I didn't know anything about the place so I went along. Gosh, it was noisy! I had only been there five minutes when a chap came over and said, "Would you like to thump the floor?" pulling me up. He literally started banging the floor with his big feet. This was not for me. He was still thumping the floor ten minutes after I came off. I never went back. Mary and Bridget thought it was a cracking night and intended going back the following weekend. However, that didn't happen. One morning in the week at 9.00am a tax inspector called to speak to them about unpaid tax and I told him they were not back yet from doing night duty, so he said he would call around midday.

When Mary and Bridget came in I gave them the message. They rushed into their room shouting, "Jesus, Mary and Joseph." They had a coffee and then rushed out of the front door. They came back late, having slept all day in the cinema. Next morning the tax inspector called again and Mrs Leberman called up to Mary and Bridget but there was no answer – they were gone. They had done a moonlight flit. Apparently that's what happened every three months. They would work for three months then scurry over to Ireland for a couple of weeks and come back to a different address.

In the other room lived a married couple. The husband was a salesman for hand dryers. Business was very poor, so there were no sales and no commission. He asked me if I could introduce him to any private nursing homes or hospitals that I knew. I suggested he should focus on all the big stores and stations. Being 1959 there were no hand dryers then, but I wish I had had the wisdom and the money to have invested in those machines –

they are everywhere now. The salesman and his wife only stayed for a month and then moved on. In the other room there was Jan from Scotland. She came knocking on my door asking for a little sugar for her coffee. Jan seemed a very likeable girl. She worked in a factory nearby. One evening Robert and I met her and she asked us if we would be interested in Wilton blankets for our bottom drawer. Seemingly there was this woman at the factory who was selling seconds at a good price. So we ordered two and she delivered them the next day. The following week we ordered another two. However, during that week, strange events were happening with Jan that made me suspicious. First, she knocked on my door holding a tray with various tins and packets on it. She asked if she could leave them with me for two hours. I said "What for?"

Then she said that social services were coming to make an inspection of her cupboards to see if she qualified for benefits and her cupboards had to be empty. Then the next morning she came with a bandage and asked me to bandage her hand because she wanted time off work. Having paid for the second order for blankets, I confronted her as two weeks had passed, and she said that the woman at the factory was waiting on a delivery. I did get one more blanket, expecting that the other one would follow, but – surprise, surprise – Jan also scampered at night, owing Mrs Leberman two weeks' rent.

We found out that the reason she had left was that she was also dealing with people in the flats fifty yards down the road. She took their money but never delivered the goods. They were very angry since there was no woman in the factory supplying the goods. It was Jan ordering from a catalogue and having them delivered to her friend's house. While all this sorry business was going on, I was working at the Manor Hospital in Golders Green. It belonged to the trade union, which meant that only TUC members were admitted. I had been in the surgical ward for a few months when I was asked to go up to Inverforth House, which was only ten minutes' walk. It was also funded by the TUC; they had decided to use it as a convalescence home. I was told it once belonged to Lord Inverforth. It was a beautiful stately home with wonderful gardens. The walls inside had superb carved oak panelling and intricately decorated ceilings.

I and three other nurses had to get the hospital all shipshape in six weeks for the opening by the Queen Mother. There was lots of unpacking linen, making beds up, unpacking all the crockery and cutlery etc. We eventually got the place looking spic and span, with one week to go before the opening. But there was a snag: we didn't have any patients to fill the beds! So a few phone calls were made to Birmingham, Manchester and Sheffield to TUC members asking if their wives were available for a visit to Golders Green. The ones who arrived were elderly and so willing to occupy the beds for the day; after all, they were going to meet the Queen Mother. The special day arrived. I, as the senior staff nurse, together with three auxiliaries, three members of the TUC and Sister from the hospital were sent up to greet the royal visitor. All the beds were full and the patients were all excited. When the car arrived we lined up at the door. The Queen Mother asked where I was from. I curtsied and said, "Scotland ma'am."

She said, "I know it well."

I then walked round with sister so that the Queen Mum could meet some of the patients. I did manage to get some photos of the Queen Mother when she drew the curtain on the plaque. That was a very special day. What I noticed about the Queen Mother was her hair: it was like spun silk – beautiful.

When the ladies had vacated the beds and gone home there was very little work to be done. We only had a few post-operative patients from the Manor Hospital. The board members came to a decision that it was too expensive to maintain this stately home and all the grounds. I think it became private flats.

I went back down to Manor Hospital for a few weeks, and then I worked for one month in Ivy House, located across the road in Golders Hill Park. It had once been the residence of Anna Pavlova, the ballerina, but now it was a male convalescence home. It was a lovely house with a huge balcony looking onto the garden and swimming pool. Inside there were pictures on the walls of all the celebrities and all the old famous film stars who had visited. Sadly the TUC had to sell that place and social services and housing took it over.

At this point, I had to ring the agency for another job. I was told to go to St Andrew's nursing home in Dollis Hill for two nights. The home was run by nuns. Most of them were Irish. When I arrived, one of the nuns told me I would be looking after a sixty-year-old man who came in for a rest. She introduced me to him; he was very softly spoken as he told me what he would like me to do. First, he would like hot milk with honey at 9.00pm, then lights out at 9.30pm. I was to wake him at 7.00am with a cup of tea – which I did. I then ran his bath and made his bed whilst he was bathing. He then went back to bed. I went off to the kitchen to get his breakfast. The nuns had their white aprons on, preparing the grapefruits so professionally, with a cherry on top. The trays, cutlery, crockery and silver tea and coffee pots were the best. They poached two perfect eggs for my man, with toast and coffee. I took it him to him and he said, "Very nice, you can go home now."

I said, "Thank you, I shall see you tonight."

So back I went and repeated all that I had done on the first night. It was the easiest job I had encountered. On the day he was leaving, I went in to wish him well and say goodbye. He said goodbye and thanked me for my kindness. I went to say goodbye to the nuns and they hoped they would see me again. As I was going out of the door one of the nuns said, "Did your man give you anything?"

I said, "No, but then I didn't do much for him."

Then she said in her Irish voice, "Sure now, your man is loaded being the Chanel No 5 man."

When I got back home to Mrs Leberman, there was a box on the doorstep with my name in large print. The lady next door told me it had been delivered by a chauffeur in a big, "posh" car. I was so excited. In the box was a large bottle of Chanel No 5 eau de toilette perfume, facial creams and cleansing lotion. There was a small card enclosed: "From a very grateful patient." What a lovely surprise.

When I rang the agency, the next address it offered was another nursing home, also run by nuns. I arrived at 8.00pm and was greeted by a very cheery nun. Mrs Smith, my patient, was waiting for me, sitting up in bed with her knees up to her chin, smoking a cigarette. She was sixty years of age, quite a frail-looking lady but with a very alert brain.

She said, "Oh, I am so glad you have arrived. Now, what's your name?"

I told her, but she wanted to know my first name so I said, "Jean," because that was what she would call me.

She told me she was a worrier and had to take sleeping pills every night, but no other medication. She did not like being on her own and asked me if I could come every night for two weeks. I said, "Yes, of course; that will fit in nicely with my arrangements" (I was going up to Scotland to spend Christmas and new year with my parents). She and Mr Smith were Scottish too and the reason they were in London was that Mr Smith was the managing director of the Allied Iron foundry and he had business and board meetings to attend. So Mrs Smith would book into a nursing home. She wasn't a hot drink person, so I settled her down for the night. She asked me if the chair was comfortable and whether I would be able to sleep. I laughed and said, "Mrs Smith, I didn't come to sleep."

But she said, "Oh, you must, Jean!"

So I said, "OK, I'll close my eyes."

In the morning, at 7.00am, I made her bed whilst she went to the bathroom. It was too early for a bath, so I went to the kitchen to collect her breakfast: scrambled egg, toast and tea. Mr Smith had arrived when I returned with the breakfast. He was around sixty-four years of age: a cheery Scotsman. He shook my hand and said, "Pleased to meet you, lass. I'm so glad you can come for two weeks."

Well, I said goodbye and off I went into the frosty air. When I arrived that night, Mrs Smith was puffing away on her cigarette with a smile on her face. I said, "Oh, you look very happy tonight." Then I saw the camp bed with pillow and duvet on the other side of her bed. I said, "What have you been up to?" And she told me that her husband's secretary had arranged it all, so that I would be more comfortable. We had nice long chats about everything in general. When I started to settle her down for the night she wouldn't lie down until I lay down. My camp bed was lower than hers and she leaned over, patted my arm and said, "Are you comfortable, Jean?"

She was such a sweet, motherly type and that's what it was like for two weeks. I enjoyed her company and she enjoyed mine.

I said to her, "You know, Mrs Smith? It feels like I am the patient, and you are the nurse!"

She laughed and said, "Now, Jean, go to sleep."

Well my two weeks were nearly up when Mr Smith came in early one morning and said to me, "Mrs Smith tells me you are going up to Scotland for Christmas and new year to see your parents. How would you like to come up with us and look after the wife for another two weeks? And spend Christmas and new year with your parents."

I said, "Yes, I would be delighted."

Although the distance between our locations in Scotland was miles, Mr Smith said he would arrange everything. Because I was having a sleep at night, Mrs Smith asked me to go to Harrods with her. So off we went in a taxi. She wanted to buy her two daughters Christmas presents. She went around whilst I sat on a chair at the side. That was my first visit to Harrods. I was amazed at the merchandise and the well-dressed customers. Soon, Mrs Smith came back, with the shop girl carrying a few bags, which I took over.

Mrs Smith then said, "Jean, have you got a travelling clock?"

I said, "No."

So off we went and she said, "Choose the one you like."

I felt so embarrassed but she insisted. I thanked her so much: I loved the clock. We got a taxi back to the nursing home and I made my way home. Friday night arrived, so I packed a few things for Mrs Smith, as she was leaving the next morning. Saturday morning dawned and I had to go home and pack. Mr Smith told me to come to the Dorchester for 5.00pm as we would be dining at 7.00pm. I just couldn't believe this was happening to me. My boyfriend, Robert, came round to see me and took me to the Tube; we said our goodbyes, then I was off to the smartest hotel in London! I asked the doorman the directions to Mr Smith's suite. Wow! I felt so grand. I knocked at the door. Mr Smith said, "Oh, you found us, lass. I've got your key and I'll take you to your room. It's just next door."

When I saw it – gosh! – a whole suite, just for me! It was beautiful. Mr Smith told me to knock at 7.00pm and we would go down to the dining room. Mrs Smith had her mink cape on and looked smart, enjoying her cigarette. I dressed smartly too. Mrs Smith asked me not to wear my uniform and that was OK by me. The dining room was huge, with long mirrors around the walls. There was a very quiet atmosphere. The waiter came with the menu: it was never-ending. I was so hungry and I didn't know what to order.

Mr Smith said, "Would you like me to order for you, lass?"

I said, "Yes please," and, "I'm not fussy with food."

He said, "We will all have the same and I'm sure you will enjoy it."

Well, I certainly did. Soup to start, white fillet of fish with a lovely sauce, fillet steak and all the trimmings ending with crème caramel. It was quite an experience sitting in front of the mirror, watching all the celebrities coming in to dine. We went up to our rooms. Mrs Smith was very tired so I said goodnight and sat looking out of my window across Hyde Park and all the Christmas lights. I set my Harrods alarm clock for 8.00am.

I slept well, as did the Smiths. Mrs Smith was going to have breakfast in bed so Mr Smith and I went down and had a delicious cooked breakfast. Mr Smith was a really down to earth man – no airs or graces. He told me he was meeting a business partner that day but he would be back for a 7.00pm dinner, then he said we would be catching the 11.00am train for Scotland the following morning. So it would be an early rise. Mrs Smith and I had a nice quiet day, with delicious sandwiches and cake for lunch in the room. Lots of magazines helped pass the time. We three had another lovely meal, and then off to bed, setting my alarm.

The next morning we went down for breakfast, our cases – all packed – were brought down by the porter and with the taxi waiting we were off to catch the train. The railway porter rushed us to our first-class compartments, mine a double next door. It was a little bit of luxury. This was my first experience of first class on a train. I always travelled second class and took a sandwich for the journey. After a good rest and a meal in the dining car we soon arrived at our destination: Falkirk. When we got off I saw a black Daimler and chauffeur waiting. The station porter brought our baggage to Henry, the chauffeur, who tipped his cap to Mr and Mrs Smith and loaded the car. What a lovely smooth journey!

We arrived at Polmont, which is a little village near Falkirk, turned up a long lane, through big gates to a large house with fields all around. Of course, these grounds all belonged to Mr Smith. We stopped at the pillared porch, where the housekeeper was standing with two of the biggest dogs I had ever seen.

They were black, shaggy German dogs. Mr Smith told me to stay in the car, then he brought the dogs over so that they could sniff me all over. He spoke to the dogs face-to-face and said "This is Jean." The dogs stepped back and Mr Smith said, "OK, lass, you can come in now." They were his guard dogs, not pets.

There was a big stone fireplace in the hall with logs burning and the two dogs sat on either side. I helped Mrs Smith up the big staircase and helped her get into bed, and then the housekeeper took me up to my room, which was really delightful. Dinner was at 7.00pm. Mrs Smith was so tired that she had hers in bed. I met the cook in the huge kitchen. Mr Smith came in with Paddy, his daughter, who had just arrived. He had another daughter, who was married with children and lived in Falkirk. Paddy was about thirty-five and was captain of a curling team, so, that being a winter sport, she was away from home most of the time. We all sat down and enjoyed a well-cooked meal. I got on really well with Paddy. She thanked me for looking after her mother and coming home with her. She was a lovely person. I didn't know what I was going to do all day because Mrs Smith would amuse herself playing patience and sleeping. When I was there a couple of days I went into her bedroom and she said, "Come and see my cameo collection."

She opened a door off her bedroom, which was her boudoir. It was filled with glass-topped cabinets with the biggest collection of cameo brooches, all displayed on green velvet. She had collected them from all over the world on her travels. I said, "Wow! Now I know why you have the guard dogs." They were spectacular.

"Oh!" she said. "That's nothing. Wait till Mr Smith shows you his collection."

The next day Mr Smith said, "Come and see my Toby jugs, lass." As soon as he took his keys out to open the door, the two dogs got up and came with him. We went into a room that looked like a big ballroom, with bars on the windows. The ceiling was high, and all around these glass-panelled walls up to the ceiling were Toby jugs. He said he had the biggest collection in the world. I believed him. I don't like Toby jugs very much – though I didn't tell Mr Smith that; he was too nice a man to offend – but it was an amazing sight when he turned the lights on. The two dogs followed us round all the time, until the door was locked, then they went back to sit at the fireplace. Paddy asked me if I would like to go Christmas shopping in Falkirk with her. I said, "I'll just go up and ask your mother it it's all right."

But Paddy said, "Oh! It was she who suggested it."

We had a lovely time. I bought a nice clock for my mother and father, and Paddy went off on her own to buy all her presents, then we met up in a lovely little tearoom.

The Christmas tree had arrived when we got back, so we helped the housekeeper to decorate it in the hall. When it was finished the hall looked so grand, with holly around the fireplace and the two dogs sitting on either side with their red collars on. They were more relaxed when Paddy was home; she would take them for long walks but Mr Smith would say, "Don't pet them now, Paddy!"

He had trained them to be good guard dogs. It was now 23 December and I was attending to Mrs Smith when she said, "Jean, why don't you go off today and spend time with your parents? But I want to ask you if you could come back for another week because Paddy will be away, as will Mr Smith, for board meetings."

So I said that, yes, that would be ok. I packed a few things and was ready to go, wondering what bus I was to get, when Mr Smith shouted, "Come on, lass, Henry's here." Wow! I couldn't believe it! I was going home in a Daimler. We arranged for Henry to come for me at 6.00pm on 2 January. I wished the Smith family a merry Christmas and a happy new year. I also said goodbye to Paddy because I would be gone when she arrived back home from her curling tour. Mr Smith handed me a brown envelope and Paddy handed me two presents. Then I sat beside Henry in the Daimler, thinking how lucky I was to have been chosen to meet such a wonderful, kind family. I felt more like a dear friend and companion to a lovely lady.

We soon arrived at my village and the miners from the village were all standing on the corner, which was a meeting place to socialise. Of course, when Henry drove in they had to peer into the car and then that would have been something to talk about. Henry said "They all know you, then?"

I said, "Oh, yes, Henry. And when you come back to collect me you will have quite an audience!"

Henry carried my case up to the door. Mum and Dad asked him in for a cup of tea but Henry declined. He later told me he never ever left the car unattended. When we walked to the gate with Henry to bid him farewell, all the neighbours were out of their gate too, shouting, "Oh my, it's like the queen's car, isn't it?" It was so good to be home. My parents just loved hearing all my news.

Christmas Day soon arrived. I got a lovely twinset from my parents, a jar of Coty face cream from Paddy, a lovely night dress from Mrs Smith and when I opened the brown envelope from Mr Smith there was £100 and my first-class train fare down to London. My parents loved the clock I bought them and £25 each, to buy what they needed. Leading up to new year I visited all my friends from the fever hospital and met their children. I had a few nights at the ballroom. It was good to meet up with friends and dancing partners. New year came and went, so I packed my case and awaited Henry on 2 January. He arrived on the dot, at 6.00. When I went out with my parents and Henry, all the neighbours were out to see me off and to see smart Henry and the Daimler. I said goodbye to Mum, Dad and my brother and waved to all the neighbours. It was a very close community then and people were like a big family unit, caring and helping one another.

We were now on our way back to Mr and Mrs Smith's. I thanked them for their very generous gifts and wrote a thank-you letter to Paddy, as I would be back in London when she came home. Mrs Smith and I spent a lovely week together and she was not so frail-looking. She took me on a visit to see her daughter and grandchildren, driven by Henry. A lovely family, but now it was time to leave I felt as if I had been on holiday with close friends. I said goodbye to the cook, and the housekeeper who was so motherly. Then Mr Smith gave me a hug and said it was a pleasure having me in his home. Last of all was Mrs Smith, who retired to bed early. I popped in and she already had tears in her eyes, as did I. We hugged and I told her I would write, which made her feel better (we did correspond, especially at Christmas, for a few years, then I heard nothing, so I don't know what happened). The housekeeper handed me a little goodie bag with delicious sandwiches and cakes for the train. Henry had the car at the door. Mr Smith and the two dogs came out to see me off. I thanked Henry for driving me around. I had a feeling of sadness but at the same time I was happy to get on the train to London because I had missed my boyfriend so much.

I got a warm welcome from my landlady; yes, she had missed me too. Next day, I rang the agency for another case. I was to take on general duties at the Hospital for Nervous Diseases at Queen Square. This meant that I would be on the staff of the NHS but getting a private wage. I would be on nights. I was on a ward where six patients were unconscious after brain surgery. They had very high temperatures so had to be tepid-sponged all night. We had fans at the side of the bed. The patients had one sheet over their naked bodies. It was a relentless job, hard and draining. I was standing on Holborn Station, waiting for a train to go home, when I started a conversation with an Irish nurse who was also working at the same hospital. Her name was Cathie. We were at Queen Square Hospital for three weeks. We became good friends and were sorry to say goodbye, hoping that we would bump into one another again. Well, we didn't see one another for eight months. I was sent to the private wing at Hendon General Hospital on nights to nurse a Jewish lady who was eighty-five years old. She was rather heavy and confused. She could not move on her own, which meant she needed two nurses during the day and two nurses at night. I was waiting to meet the other night nurse and, lo and behold, she turned out to be Cathie – who eventually became my future sister-in-law. I was very pleased to see her again. We were in Hendon Hospital for one week, when the family wanted to take their mother home, so they asked us if we would come home with her. Of course, Cathie and I accepted and the family residence was not far from the hospital.

The house was three-bedroomed and semi-detached. The patient lived with her two elderly sons. The rest of the family were married and lived close by. Mrs Kamovski, our patient, had to be turned, with pressure areas treated every two hours. She always wanted to be left alone. She reminded me of an elderly Greta Garbo. The family were Orthodox Jews so they fasted for Hanukkah, which meant there was no food for Cathie or me. There were plenty of matzo biscuits, but that was all. All the other food had been thrown out. We had lots of cups of tea, so when the two day nurses arrived, Cathie and I hurried along to a nice café at the Tube station and had a delicious breakfast, which we put on the bill at the end of the week. When we were washing the old lady, making her bed and even feeding her breakfast, she would make quite a fuss and shout, "Leave me alone, I vant to sleep!" Sometimes she would pretend to be deeply asleep and not respond to questions. Cathie and I knew all her wily ways.

We had been there for two weeks and when we arrived one particular night we were confronted with the whole family in the hall – most of them crying. Cathie and I thought she had passed on. The nurse and eldest son told us she was unconscious and it didn't look good. Cathie and I went into the room to see her and she looked pretty good to us, so we had our doubts about her being in a coma. She would respond to our voice so I just put my hand under the cover and gently pinched her plump thigh. She immediately shouted, "What are you doing? I vant to sleep."

Well, the family could not believe what they were hearing. They thought it was a miracle and asked what we had done to their mother. So we had to tell them that their mother was a devious old lady and she just wanted to be in charge and be left alone. After a few more weeks, the eldest son told us one night that the finances were not looking healthy and they couldn't pay for four nurses. However, they found a reasonably priced nursing home for their mother.

My friend Cathie was going back to Ireland to get married. Her fiancé lived near her home and she had known him since her school days. We took a couple of days off from cases because we had to go shopping for a wedding dress. I was very happy for Cathie, but at the same time I felt sad because I would miss her as a very good friend. My boyfriend and I decided to have a farewell night out with Cathie. However, Robert's brother Ronnie asked if he could join us. When we met up and introduced Cathie to Ronnie it was amazing how the meeting between the two of them turned out. It was as if they had met before, or knew one another; Cathie even said to me, "I feel as if I have known Ron before."

She was so thankful that Ron had come that evening because that was the start of a big romance. Within a week of them meeting, Cathie knew that the wedding in Ireland had to be called off.

Now it was back to work. My next case was in a block of flats in St John's Wood. I was to nurse a Greek lady – seventy-two years of age – living with her niece and nephew. I arrived at 8.00pm and the flat was lit by many candles. I introduced myself and discovered that they couldn't speak a word of English. They took me into the bedroom, where there were two empty beds. I wondered where the patient was, but then I heard a groan and heavy breathing. At first I felt uneasy, then I looked behind the door, where I found the Greek lady slumped in an armchair. She was a big lady and looked very ill. The reason she was in the chair was because her breathing felt better when upright rather than being in bed. I couldn't believe she had been in the chair for three months. The chair had been adapted like a commode. But the poor lady had developed fluid in her tissues, causing a lot of pressure and wedging her in the chair. The only word the old lady could say was "fan". I was a bit baffled until I saw a Spanish fan on the dressing table. I started fanning the patient's face and she kept nodding her head up and down, meaning that was what she wanted. She soon drifted off to sleep so I slipped into the kitchen for a cup of tea and toast. The niece and nephew returned to bed. When I went back into the bedroom her breathing had become very laboured and her pulse a lot weaker. I rang the GP and gave him the report. He said he would be with me in half an hour. The doorbell rang and as I went to the frosted glass door I could see the shape of a man that reminded me of a Sandeman Port bottle. When I opened the door the GP introduced himself with a very Scottish accent as Dr McPherson. He wore a long black cape, a black wide-brimmed hat and sported long side whiskers. He agreed that the lady had deteriorated and did not have long to live, so I made a cup of tea and we waited for a life to end. He told me the niece and nephew did not want to be present at the end.

The final end was at 2.00am. The doctor and I decided to get the old lady out of the chair and lay her on the bed. It was quite a struggle, as we had to break the two chair arms to release the patient. We were thankful that the bed was low as it was easier to lay her on the bed. The doctor thanked me for making her so presentable for the niece and nephew and then he left. I waited until the niece and nephew woke up around 7.30am and informed them of the sad news. They took it very well and were so pleased to see their aunt lying peacefully in bed. I wrote out my expense sheet but they brushed it aside and handed me fifty pounds. They wanted me to accept it – so I did, with gratitude. I made them toast and tea before the "Sandeman doctor" came to see them. When he arrived, I said my farewells and headed for home. I rang the agency and informed them about my Greek lady passing away. Miss Hill gave me the address of my next case. He was a fifty-year-old man who had come out of hospital after having a hernia repaired. The house was in Golders Green. The gentleman was up and about and doing well. Miss Hill said that his wife just wanted a rest from attending to all his needs. She also told me that his nurse had left to go on holiday to Ireland.

I slept well and made my way to Golders Green at 7.00pm. I got off the bus and was met by four ladies, asking if I was the nurse from Hill's agency. I said I was, and they introduced themselves as the wife, two daughters and the grandma. I thought it was strange having a welcome like that. The house was only walking distance from the bus terminal and the family seemed very friendly. I was expecting to see the patient when I arrived but he was missing. Then Mrs Lohan, the wife said, "Oh, I shall take you upstairs to meet my husband." I thought he had retired early to bed. Well, we went up one flight of stairs (which was where the bedrooms were), but the wife started up the next flight to the attic room. I couldn't believe what I was seeing when she opened the door. My eyes had to adjust to the dimly lit room. There was a lamp on the floor with a bulb the size of a cherry. I looked for a bed but couldn't see one. Then the wife went behind the door and said, "This is my husband." He was lying on a mattress on the floor in a foetal position.

I got down on my knees to get a close-up of his condition and discovered he was a very ill man. I spoke to the wife about the information that I had received from the agency – which was wrong. She told me it was so difficult hiring a nurse that she had to tell little lies. Her husband was in a deep sleep, so she took me downstairs to show me around. She asked me what time I wanted to have my break. So I said midnight would be fine. So she said she would leave me some nourishment in the kitchen and she would come and relieve me.

I went back up to the attic and the patient was awake, asking for his injection of morphine. I had to use a large torch to read the medication instructions from the doctor. I asked the lady of the house for a larger bulb but was told that her husband did not like a brighter light. So I had to work with a torch to do everything for the patient. I had a feeling that I was in for a dismal night. I knew the patient had cancer – and that it was terminal – without reading the doctor's file. Morphine was to be given every three to four hours. Turning him from side to side was so difficult when I was on my knees. It was soon midnight and I was ready for a cup of tea and whatever little delicacy had been left out in the kitchen. The wife came in her dressing gown and told me not to be long.

When I entered the kitchen, I was shocked when I saw the "tasty" morsel on the plate. It was a piece of battered fish that was rock hard and when I tapped it on the plate it broke in half with no fish inside. On the table was one slice of caraway seed bread (which I am not partial to). There were two teaspoons of tea, two ounces of milk and a small portion of butter. I went to the fridge to see if I could find an egg and different bread, but – lo and behold – the fridge had a padlock on it. Well, that took the biscuit! I wasn't surprised that the previous nurses had left at short notice. I made myself a cup of tea when the lady of the house called down asking if I was finished – I had been downstairs for just fifteen minutes. When I went upstairs, she was closing her own bedroom door. I had made up my mind in the kitchen that I could not endure another night looking after this poor man, who should have been in a hospital or a nursing home. I made out my expense sheet for one night, which was around £7 including fares and a meal that was inedible. I came downstairs at 8.00, after making the patient comfortable and giving him his injection. The lady of the house said, "Oh! You can't go yet! Not until the day nurse comes."

I informed her that I only do twelve hours and handed her my bill. She said, "What's this?"

So I told her that her husband should be in hospital and that I would not be coming back. So she looked at my bill and tore it up. I told her the agency would get in touch with her. Well, I said goodbye and was so glad to get out into a fresh sunny morning. I walked straight to a nice little café at the bus terminal and had a delicious breakfast. When I arrived home, my landlady told me the agency had been ringing, so I knew that Mrs Lohan had contacted the agency. When Miss Hill rang again, she sounded very cross with me, but then I told her my side of the story and she was very upset that she had been lied to and therefore given me the wrong information about the patient. Miss Hill said she would send another bill and would not supply a nurse to go to the house. I was finally paid. The patient passed away one week later in a nursing home.

My next case was one of the most frightening ones I have experienced. The address was a flat in Kensington Court. I was employed for night nurse duties. I arrived at this large apartment and took the lift up to the fourth floor, where I stood at a part-frosted glass door; the other part was a panel of cardboard. I thought, "Oh dear: a nasty accident."

I rang the doorbell and a seventy-year-old, well-spoken, white-haired lady came to the door. I noticed she had a bandage on her arm. I introduced myself, wondering if she was my patient, Alice, but she said, "Oh no, I'm the aunt." She then explained to me about Alice, her niece, who was nineteen years of age and had been in a very deep depression since her father passed away two years previously. She showed me a beautiful framed photo of her niece, pretty and smiling. I asked the aunt what was wrong with her arm; she seemed to just brush it away and said, "Oh it's nothing, it will be better soon."

So I then asked her what my duties would be for Alice. She said, "Well, there isn't very much for you to do, but I just want you to be here – just to watch over Alice when she comes out of the bedroom." She then told me that Alice had taken over her father's bedroom since he passed away, and the only time she came out was when she was hungry.

The father and Alice had been very close since the mother had left the marriage. They rode their horses along Rotten Row every weekend and went on many holidays together. Alice did not allow anyone into the bedroom. The aunt told me that if Alice came out of the bedroom that night and asked who I was, I had to say I was there to look after the aunt. The aunt then took me into the kitchen and showed me where everything was. The fridge was well stocked with food; there was a whole chicken and lots of fresh salad. I was invited to help myself for my meal at midnight. She showed me a small room with a bed. The aunt said that if I felt tired I could come in and lie down, but I had to remember to lock the door, because it was Alice's room and she might decide to come back – which was doubtful after two years. The aunt then said goodnight. I read some magazines in the sitting room, which was very cosy, with an electric fire. It was soon midnight and I was ready for something to eat. I listened at Alice's door and all was quiet, so I made my way to the kitchen. I put the kettle on, took the chicken out of the fridge and a carving knife from the cutlery drawer. I buttered some bread and prepared some salad. I thought I heard a creaky floorboard but carried on fixing my salad on the plate when this voice said, "Who are you?"

I turned round and nearly jumped ten feet in the air. There was a girl standing at the kitchen door. I presumed that this was Alice and she was not the pretty girl I saw in the picture frame. She looked so frightening. In a trembling voice I said, "Oh, hello

67

– you must be Alice. I'm Jean and I am here to care for you aunt."
I asked her if she would like something to eat but she didn't
answer me. But suddenly she came over, picked up the carving
knife and stabbed the whole chicken through the middle and
marched off to her bedroom with it. I felt like the jelly in the
fridge. I quickly put cheese between two slices of bread on my
salad plate, poured a cup of tea and quickly vacated the kitchen
to the small bedroom, locking the door behind me.

I was in the bedroom about one hour when I heard the door
handle rattling. My heart was pounding like Thumper's foot
in *Bambi*. I kept really quiet and eventually Alice went back to
her room. In the morning I waited until the aunt was up and
about. Then I heard her talking to someone who turned out to
be the day nurse. When the aunt was getting dressed, the day
nurse filled me in with the trouble that Alice was causing the
flat dwellers. It was Alice who had broken the glass door and she
had attacked the aunt and bitten her arm. The neighbours were
complaining about the noise. The aunt was trying to protect
Alice and prevent her from being sectioned by her psychiatrist,
the day the nurse told me to be on guard. I told her about the
incident in the kitchen with the chicken. I explained that I didn't
think I would be back that night. When I told the aunt, she was
very understanding, and asked, "If I got a friend to come in and
sit with you, would you come?" I said that, yes, I would be OK
with that arrangement.

I arrived that night at 7.00pm. The aunt said that Alice had
probably eaten all the chicken and so she didn't think she would
be hungry that night. I was glad that the room Alice was in
was en suite. The aunt told me her friend would ring the bell
around 11.00. She said goodnight and retired to her bedroom at
10.00pm. One hour passed and then the doorbell rang. I jumped
up to welcome the aunt's friend. When I opened the door the
friend was gasping for breath, looked purple and was unsteady
on his feet. He introduced himself as Jeffrey. He had known the

family for years and had known Alice as a toddler. Well, Jeffrey turned out to be so friendly and interesting. I couldn't believe he was ninety years old. He had slept a few hours during the day so that he wouldn't fall asleep on me. We went into the kitchen, where I made lots of sandwiches with delicious ham, lettuce and tomatoes. I made a pot of tea and cut two pieces of cake. I carried everything into the front room and we had a lovely feast. We didn't hear a sound from Alice's room. The night passed quickly. Jeffrey waited until the aunt got up. I got his coat and helped him get ready for the road. We said goodbye and he said, "See you tonight."

As Jeffrey was going out of the door, the day nurse was coming in. I then wrapped myself up and got ready for my journey home. I had a nice hot bath and then prepared breakfast before I jumped into bed. As I was drifting off to sleep my landlady shouted up that I had a telephone call. I ran downstairs and it was the day nurse to tell me that Alice had gone "berserk" and she was being sectioned. So I would not be required any more. I felt so sorry for the aunt. She had done her best to keep Alice safe in her flat instead of being locked up. I think she was hoping for a miracle. So I rang the agency and told them I would be taking two days off so that I could spend some time with my beloved.

My next job was for day duties at a nursing home called Greenways. Mrs Galt was the matron and most of the staff were Irish between thirty and forty years of age. Peter was a male nurse and Fred was a waiter and porter. They were in a relationship and lived together. They didn't refer to their stance as a gay couple – they used the word "queer" in the year 1960. They were a very nice couple and very comical. I was here to nurse a thirty-year-old, famous *Queen* magazine model. She was beautiful, elegant and over six feet tall. She had beautiful clothes but she just could not stop crying. She had been in a very deep depression and was now suicidal. She had been on strict sedation day and night, but was now being weaned off the sedation. I have never seen anyone cry buckets like she did. When I brought her meal tray up from the kitchen, her plate would fill up with tears. She had a bath every day and just sat there and cried. She couldn't do anything for herself. I had to wash her all over, dry her and comb her hair. She was like a child.

Her husband came to visit on the third day. It was all very businesslike on his side, but she was so pleased to see him and was very loving. In fact, she wanted to go home with him but he sharply said, "No not yet!"

Of course, she started crying so much – the husband just got up and left. I was with her for two weeks and she was looking to me for guidance on what she should wear and whether her make-up was good. I could see an improvement in her well-being, with not so much crying. Her doctor came in one day and suggested that I take her out to the cinema or the hairdresser's. Well, she opted to have her hair done. So, the next day I rang for a taxi, which was on call at any time for the nursing home. I gave the address to the cab driver, which was in the City of London. So off we went. She had her hair done and the staff all knew her and who she was. She went off to the ladies' while I got in touch with the taxi driver to take us back. The taxi arrived but she was gone; she had just disappeared. Then one of the staff said,

"Oh, I'll bet she has gone to see her husband, who has an office not far from here."

I got the address, jumped into the taxi and went round to his office. She was there – crying and pleading with him. He was furious with me for not keeping an eye on her. But, as I told him, I was not aware of a back door in the hairdresser's. When we got back to the nursing home, I told her never to do that again because I was worried. She apologised to me and said she would behave like a grown-up. The following week I decided to take her to the cinema. I rang the taxi driver for 1.00pm to go to the matinee. We had lunch and the taxi driver arrived.

Finchley Road traffic was very busy at any time of the day. We were crawling along the busy road when all of a sudden the taxi door swung open and this elegant model jumped out and started running down the pavement, with arms flailing and legs going in all directions. I jumped out after her and shouted to the cabbie to "Follow us up!"

After I caught up with her, she stopped and started crying and apologising. We got back into the taxi and returned to the nursing home. I certainly did not want to take her into a darkened cinema in the state she was in. I was with her another week and then she left the nursing home with a friend and not her husband. I just hope that she recovered without him.

My next patient was a Mrs Todd, in the same nursing home. I was taken to her room to be introduced. She was sitting up in bed like an Egyptian mummy, all bandaged around the head. She was on a liquid diet through a straw. It was an effort for her to speak. I was then told she had had a facelift. This was a word that wasn't really heard of in 1960. My duties were just to bring her food tray and escort her to the bathroom. The head had to be kept upright. She told me her husband was coming in later to visit. As I was coming back from my lunch the main doorbell rang. I went to answer it and standing before me was Richard Todd, a very famous English film star. He was very tanned and very handsome, with a lovely smile. He said he had come to visit his wife, Mrs Todd. I said, "Oh, I'm the nurse looking after your wife, sir."

And he said, "Good; how is she, nurse?"

The only answer I could give him was resting and comfortable. I took him down to the room and left. Mrs Todd was in for one week. I didn't know what she looked like before her facelift and I didn't know if it was a success, because she left late at night with her husband, so I didn't get the pleasure of seeing Richard Todd one more time. I think he was given a knighthood in the early Eighties.

The nursing home was a very busy place with lots of comings and goings of famous people. Most of the patients who came into Greenways were stressed, depressed, mentally exhausted or suicidal. When they left, their departures were always in the dark, when no reporters or photographers were around. Mrs Galt, the matron, sent for me and asked me to come in the next day as she was expecting a VIP and she wanted me to attend to him. I had to wait until morning to find out who it was. When I found out it was Tony Hancock I was so excited to see him in the flesh. He was the biggest TV comedian in those days. I went up and introduced myself. He came over to me as a very shy man. He explained to me that he did not wear any nightwear in bed and asked whether I would mind. I said that, no, it didn't bother me. I was told that he was in for a rest and also that he had been drinking too much. He was on sedation, but it was not having much effect. When I brought his meal tray he would then say, "Where's the wine?" with a little side grin expression that he did quite a lot on TV.

His tipple was Beaujolais and quite often he would ask me to go down to the matron, to tell her he had been a very good chap and thought he deserved a glass of Beaujolais – but the doctor left strict orders. One day Sid James put his head round the door and said, "Wotcha," followed by a gurgling laugh. All Tony wanted to know was, "Did he bring a bottle?"

The toilet was just outside the door to the left, so when Tony wanted to go I would be on the lookout. He would run out on his tiptoes and run back. He didn't even like putting on a dressing gown. One morning I went down for his coffee tray; I had to go down four flights of stairs to the kitchen but I only got as far as the first flight when I heard screams coming from Tony's direction. I ran up to see Tony in the nude, standing in a female patient's room, standing like a boy scout with his right hand covering his privates and the left hand saluting, saying, "I beg your pardon." He had taken the wrong turning for the toilet.

Tony just said, "Sorry, lost my direction! No harm done, now where is my bottle?"

At this time of his life he had separated from his wife and was engaged to Freddie, his female agent. She was very attractive but when she came to visit it was all rather businesslike. The following year I was doing a few nights at Greenways relieving staff holiday when we got a call late at night to say that Tony was coming in. Well, I nearly cried when I saw him; he looked so unwell. He had the shakes and was also having epileptic seizures. His relationship with Freddie had also deteriorated. However, under medication and good nursing, he recovered enough to go home. A few years later I read in a paper that he wanted to make a hit in Australia, but he went on his own and I think loneliness contributed to his suicide in a hotel in Australia. The public had lost a big star.

Another big star was to enter Greenways – Judy Garland. My agency rang me to say that the matron wanted to know if I was available to nurse her that night. I was so excited – wondering what she was like and what was wrong with her. Well I arrived at 7.00pm and had to wait until 10.00pm before she came in. Her two doctors half carried her in from the car. She had a blanket round her and a big scarf covering her head. She had attempted suicide again. She had taken pills but not enough to warrant a stomach pump. The doctors managed to get her up the stairs. There were no lifts in this nursing home, but then it was two big houses knocked into one many years previously. I had the bed turned down all ready for Judy. I couldn't believe her appearance when we took the blanket and scarf from her. She looked dishevelled and her hair needed washing. The doctors just wanted me to put her into bed and offer drinks of water if she woke up. She was already in her night attire, so that was easy because she was half asleep anyway.

She slept all night and at 6.00am she said, "Where am I?"

I said, "You are in Greenway nursing home, Miss G."

Then she asked me my name, I said that it was Nurse Shaw but she wanted my first name. So I said, "Jean."

She then asked "Jean, have you gotta comb?"

I said, "Yes."

"Well, could I borrow it, please?"

So Judy Garland tried to comb her hair but wasn't making any progress. So I said, "Here, let me help you." I made her hair a bit more presentable than it was.

She said, "You are very kind, Jean, now can you ring for a taxi for me?"

"Oh!" I said. "You have to have breakfast first, Miss G."

She said OK, that she would have coffee and toast. I noticed that she had very small limbs compared with her body. I rang down to the office, to let them know that Miss G was awake and ask whether someone could come up whilst I went down to the kitchen to get her breakfast. When I brought the tray up it was time for me to go home. I said goodbye and didn't think I would be seeing Judy Garland again. I was wrong, because about two months later the agency rang me and said the doctors wanted the same nurse that had looked after Miss Garland to come to Kensington Mews that morning at 9.00 – so off I went.

As I turned up the street, I was looking at the buildings and the door numbers. My eyes happened to look up at one of the windows and who was sitting smoking his cigar but Winston Churchill. Judy Garland's residence was about four doors further along. I rang the bell and an elderly women answered; she turned out to be the housekeeper. I stepped into the hall and it was like Piccadilly Circus. I was amazed at the number of people just standing in the hall, all talking to one another: four doctors, a personal agent, a housekeeper, a maid, a cook, a teacher, a nursemaid and two other nurses in uniform. The two children, Joey and Lorna, were there – but not Liza – she was with her father in the USA. Suddenly Judy came down the stairs, shouting for the agent to ring Sam Spiegel, who was a top director in Hollywood. The agent told Judy that he would be sound asleep in LA with the time difference. Whilst all this was going on, one of the doctors called me over and told me that, because Judy was suicidal, I had to go up to her room and look for any drugs. Well, I had had to do this chore with another patient's bedroom. I searched the corners of the carpets and found nothing, then the hems of the curtains – and sure enough I felt a bulky little stash of pills. Mission completed just in time. As Judy came up the stairs she shouted, "And I don't want any nurses in my bedroom."

So I went into the kitchen for a coffee. I asked the doctor if I would be required for tomorrow; the answer was yes, but there was a possibility that they might be off to America. Well, I spent the day just chatting to the housekeeper and maid and doing nothing. I got my account book to write down my expenses bill. When I went along the next morning the hall was packed with luggage and four boxes. I gave my expenses bill to her agent, hoping he would deal with it straight away, but he just put it in his pocket. I didn't know I would have to wait about two months before I got paid. I had to send three bills to Hollywood Studios. The amount was only about £26 – around £7 per day – plus fares. I added the stamp price to send to America. I certainly didn't work for nothing! I received the exact amount – no apology, no note – just a cheque.

The agency had another case for me at Greenways again. This time it was to look after Penelope Mortimer. She was the wife of John Mortimer, the writer of the *Rumpole* series on TV. She was an author too. When I went to introduce myself, she said she only wanted me to serve her with her meals, run her bath and make her bed. She also told me she was writing a book. Years later, the book was a bestseller and a big box office film starring Peter Finch. The film was *The Pumpkin Eater*. One morning I had just brought her breakfast in when the door opened and her husband put his head round to say good morning. Penelope picked up a small vase of flowers and threw it at the door. It missed him; he knew he was not welcome and left. I didn't see him again.

Penelope was only at Greenways to have the peace and quiet to write her book. I don't know why she was so hostile to her husband. He was very nice and polite. However, later on, they were divorced and John Mortimer was knighted. It was revealed that he was unfaithful throughout his marriage and that he fathered a child with Wendy Craig, the actress on TV. So this explains the hostility. I was with Penelope for two weeks and then it was time for a break. So my boyfriend and I went down to the coast for two weeks. It was lovely to get the sea air.

I had a break from the Greenway nursing home and was sent to Miriam Moses, who was eighty years of age. She had been a Justice of the Peace and had also founded a Jewish Brady girls' club. She had had an operation and was doing well, but needed someone to go home with her to convalesce. I agreed to go for two weeks to her flat in St John's Wood. She was a lovely lady – warm and friendly. Then I met Miriam's niece, the day we were leaving the hospital. She introduced herself as the niece – no name. She had a rather cold and abrupt manner so I didn't warm to her. She then told Miriam that, instead of going to Miriam's flat, we were going to stay at her flat. The niece was very overweight and she definitely "wore the trousers" in the house. The husband was small and wore very thick glasses. He had not much to say about the set-up. Miriam would rather have gone to her own flat but she didn't want to cause any unpleasantness so we decided to go along with her arrangements. I had a feeling there was a motive behind it all. The niece showed me around the flat and took me into the kitchen. I knew they were very Orthodox Jews when I saw the kitchen. It was quite spacious, with a dividing line right down the middle: one half was blue for the fish and dairy produce and the other half was red for kosher meat. There were two cookers, two sinks, red and blue tea towels and separate cupboards for the crockery and cutlery. The niece told me that if I heated up some milk for Miriam I was not to pass over the line into the red area: I got the message.

I went in and told Miriam I had been lectured about the dos and don'ts and she said, "God, she does go over the top, don't worry about her!"

Of course, I knew about the Sabbath and the lighting of candles at sunset on Fridays until sunset Saturday, but I didn't know that the light switches could not be turned on and off. So, when I went into the kitchen to get a drink, I switched the light on and then the husband came in and went berserk shouting, "You turned the light on!"

I said, "Sorry, I'm finished now – you can turn the light off!"

Then he shouted, "You do it, you do it!" Well, I didn't know about that little ritual. I was learning all the time.

I had been there a few days and Miriam was doing well. She liked her two hours' "shut-eye" in the afternoon, after lunch. I would just sit in Miriam's room and either write letters or look at some magazines, but the niece had other things on her mind to use up my time. "As you are washing up Miriam's dishes, could you wash all the dishes?"

I said, " I don't mind helping out, but not every day."

The kitchen was always full of dirty dishes, pots and pans on the blue and red sides. She cooked lots of fish in batter to last the week and cakes for her bridge sessions.

One day when I arrived she handed me a white frilly maid's apron and told me she would like me to wheel the tea trolley in and serve tea to her bridge guests. Well, that was the last straw. I told her I was not a domestic and I was not there for her benefit. Now I knew what her motive was. When I told Miriam, she was angry; she was going to have a word with her, but I said, "No, we will just forget about it," as I only had about another week to go.

The week flew past and Miriam had recovered well and was much stronger. The day I left, the niece handed me a present all wrapped up in nice gift paper. I thought this was too good to be true. I had said goodbye to Miriam and was ready to go out of the front door but decided to go to the bathroom before I left. I opened the present and it was only one of her big nightdresses with a big hole in it! Well, I screwed it up into a ball, came out and threw it into her bedroom where she was standing. I was so glad I opened it, because I destroyed the pleasure she would have had thinking she had humiliated me in my own house. The following week Miriam was on television. She was chosen for *This Is Your Life*, presented by Eamonn Andrews.

I rang the agency for another case and Miss Hill asked me to go to King Edward VII hospital, where mostly royals and senior military personnel were treated. I asked who the patient was but the matron said she would give me all the details when I arrived. It wasn't too far from Baker Street Tube station. When I got there, I saw this tiny grey-haired woman with a navy uniform and a tall, frilly cap, who turned out to be the matron. She could only have been about four feet four inches. She showed me to the locker room, where I could put my belongings, then she said, "Now I shall take you up to the duke."

This turned out to be the Duke of Gloucester, the Queen's uncle. I asked the matron what my duties were to be and I was informed that, as she had a lot of staff on annual leave, I was to take his meals and assist him in and out of bed, make his bed and arrange all the flowers that were arriving; I was just to call him "sir". I was a little bit nervous at first, but when I met him he was quiet and was always reading. I was with him about two days and was just going in to say good morning to His Royal Highness when Sir Douglas Fairbanks Junior came out of the room opposite. He had his satin dressing gown on and, boy, did he have a great tan.

He said, "Good morning; how's the duke?" with a charming smile.

I said, "He is very well, thank you." Wow! I never thought I would see another famous film star – and so good looking!

The staff in this hospital had been there for years and they were so snooty and full of themselves. They were all on first-name terms with one another and with the patients. This would be unheard of in the NHS. I was informed by Audrey that the Queen Mother was coming to visit the duke that day at midday, and that there was no need for me to hang around. I was furious and said, "Excuse me, Audrey. I don't hang around for anybody, but when it is the Queen Mother I will be standing by the door. The duke is my patient and – by the way – I have met and spoken to the Queen Mother before, you know."

Well, the Queen Mother arrived. I opened the door and curtsied. She said, "Thank you, nurse," and then I left.

The duke was in hospital for investigations, so I was only there for another day. I didn't make my bill out to the royals; I was paid by the matron. I said my farewells but I didn't know I would be seeing them all again in about one month, but Greenway nursing home needed me for one night to look after an old lady of eighty years, called Mrs Delves Broughton. I was told she was the sister of Sir Compton McKenzie, a famous author in Scotland who wrote the book for the film *Whisky Galore*.

My old lady had a daughter who was also an author. She had quite a few books on the shelf. I forgot what her first name was because I didn't hear it spoken very often. The mother called her Little Owl and she called her mother Owl – a most peculiar twosome: very eccentric. Funnily enough, both had very sharp pointed noses that represented beaks. The daughter told me the old lady had been off her food and the only thing she wanted to eat was "bengers", which was like glutenous porridge that was sieved. Babies were weaned on it and it was very nutritious. The chef didn't have time to make this for her, so I had to make a huge bowl of it every morning. She had a bowl of this every three hours. She had sugar on it and she loved it. I was with her for a week and then the daughter asked me to go home with them to their cottage in Kent. I said I would, so we all hopped into the shooting brake and the daughter drove us down. When we arrived at the cottage it looked "olde worlde" but when we got inside – oh dear! It was dark, gloomy and hadn't seen a daily cleaner for months. I started upstairs, to make the Owl's bed with clean sheets so she could get into it straight away. Little Owl put the kettle on for a much-longed-for cup of tea. I did feel sorry for them both, so after I made Owl comfortable and gave her some bengers I started on the kitchen; it was a mess and needed a good clean. The cottage hadn't been maintained for years; some windows were cracked and the kitchen cabinets were old and had hinges falling off. I suppose they just didn't get round to getting all these jobs done – because the money was there. Little Owl went out for our supper – fish and chips. I laid the table and she lit the candles. I didn't have the heart to tell her that I didn't care much for candlelight when I was eating. I think it's more the smell then the lighting effect that I don't like.

Around 7.00pm Little Owl informed me that I would be sleeping in a neighbour's cottage 100 yards down the road, so she took me down there and introduced me. It was very nice and comfortable. I slept well. The lady of the house brought me a cup of tea in the morning. I got dressed and made my way over to the Owl's barn. It had been a cold night and the Delves Broughton cottage was pretty chilly; however, the daughter had a nice breakfast ready with a lovely aroma of coffee, but I made a pot of tea for myself. The old girl had her bengers and then I gave her a thorough bed bath and made her comfortable. It was the same routine for the week. It was soon time to leave; I said my farewells and the daughter drove me to the train station, which wasn't too far away. I was soon back in my home with a few days off.

After having a good rest and spending nice days with my beloved it was time to go back to work. I was soon back at Greenways to nurse the millionairess Olga Deterding. She was suicidal at the time, so had to be watched every minute of the night. She could only have been around thirty years of age and was very depressed. She had been besotted with Albert Schweitzer, who did a lot of missionary work in Africa. Olga used to follow him around, but she was also donating all her money to his projects. When the family got to know about it, they brought her back to England and then depression set in. She had both wrists bandaged but they were on the mend. The family were very cross that she was handing out her inheritance. She did recover eventually and left the nursing home in better shape than when she came in. At that time there was a programme on TV called *Whicker's World* and Alan Whicker was presenting a cruise on the *Queen Elizabeth II* liner. On the cruise was Olga, who met up with Alan Whicker and they got engaged, but it was called off for some reason not disclosed to the public.

My next appointment was back at King Edward VII Hospital to nurse a General Frederick Browning. He was a very nice man and reminded me of General Montgomery. He was undergoing a few investigations. He was in overall charge of all the domestics at Buckingham Palace. His wife came into visit him and she introduced herself as Daphne du Maurier. I shook her hand and said, "How do you do?"

I was so pleased to have met her; she was so charming and a beautiful woman. I only stayed for four days with the general, as the tests proved negative and he went home.

The next assignment was to go to a flat off the Edgware Road and nurse a terminally ill patient. He was in his late forties and very poorly. I rang the bell and the wife answered the door. She was a very striking lady, beautifully dressed, with stunning jewellery and her hair carefully styled. It was 7.30pm, so I presumed she was going out for the evening. She introduced me to the housekeeper cook, who looked like Mrs Bridges in *Upstairs, Downstairs*. Then she took me upstairs to meet the day nurse, who finished at 8.00pm. There was a large, beautiful, russet-coloured poodle lying outside the bedroom door. The nurse came out to give me the report on the patient, which was not good: it was only a matter of time. He was slipping into unconscious. The lady of the house did go out for the evening. I said goodnight to the day nurse. The housekeeper showed me what food there was for me in the kitchen. I was just told to help myself. She retired early to her room for the night. I was there to make this gentleman as comfortable as possible. He resembled Sir Mortimer Wheeler from the 1950s *Animal, Vegetable, Mineral?* TV show. He looked like he had been a very handsome man in his day, with his mass of red hair and moustache. He was no weight, so I had to treat his pressure areas and turn him every two hours. I did manage to give him sips of water. Her Ladyship arrived home around 2.00am. She called in to ask if everything was all right and then she said goodnight. Next morning the day nurse arrived at 8.00am and I was ready to go home, but the housekeeper called me into the kitchen and told me to sit down and have some breakfast with her, so we sat down to scrambled eggs on toast – just like my mother used to make. Just as I was getting my coat on, the lady of the house came down in her dressing gown and told the housekeeper that Princess Margaret was calling for her at 7.00pm. This lady was seemingly on the board of a large charity organisation, and a big evening event was being held that night. So I asked, "Could I come earlier tonight to see Princess Margaret arrive from the lounge room window?"

And Her Ladyship said, "Yes, of course."

I was looking forward to seeing the big car arriving with HRH. I rang the bell at 6.30pm and the day nurse opened the door to inform me that the patient had passed away ten minutes before I came and the wife had rung Buckingham Palace to cancel the meeting with HRH. I didn't think I would be needed that night, but the wife came down all dressed with her coat and gloves on ready to go out. She asked me to stay for the night and she would see me in the morning. The day nurse went home and I went in to see "Mrs Bridges" in the kitchen, where she had made a pot of tea. The taxi came for Her Ladyship: she was spending the night with her sister. I could hear the poor dog quietly whining upstairs so I went up to the landing and there he was lying outside his master's door. He wouldn't come to me so I left him to grieve. The cook made me a lovely salad for midnight and sandwiches for later on, then she retired to bed.

I had lots of magazines to read so the night soon passed. The cook was up at 7.00am and Her Ladyship arrived back at 8.00am. I said how sorry I was for her loss.

She said, "Thank you… do you want a dog?"

I replied, "Pardon?"

Then she said again, "Would you like my husband's dog?"

"Oh!" I said. "He's absolutely gorgeous, but I live in a rented room in a private house, so it wouldn't be possible."

She said, "He's top pedigree!"

I responded, "Yes and he looks it."

He had the loveliest coat and the colour was superb. I expect he had a top clipper and groomer – the same one used for the corgis in Buckingham Palace. Well, I had breakfast with the cook in the kitchen, said my goodbyes and that was the end of a very short case.

It was now 1962 and it was time to introduce my fiancé to my mother and father. So we drove all the way up to Scotland. We had a lovely week up there. My mum, dad and family were so pleased to see us and made Robert very welcome. We decided to marry the following year. But we had to think about saving up for a mortgage for a house. We went to the building society but they did not take a female's income into account. However, one of them asked me what my job was and I said that it was nursing. He then asked how long I intended working. I said that it would be quite a few years. So they agreed to put us in their books to look for a house.

We spent weekends going around looking at houses on the

market. During the week I worked in Greenways and other nursing homes. So I was doing general duties relieving and filling in for staff on holiday and sick leave. Finally, we saw a three-bedroom terraced house for £3,500. It was on an attractive small street with lovely gardens. Also, no cars were parked on the road. The elderly couple were moving to the coast and the house would be vacant the following month. So that meant that I would have to say goodbye to Mrs Leberman and George and move into our own house. The house wasn't too distant from Mrs Leberman so I could visit sometimes when I had a day off.

We decided to marry in Scotland, which meant we had to visit the minister who would marry us, but we had to live there for one week before he was able to call the banns. Another chapter was beginning in my life that was very exciting.

I am so fortunate to have a very good memory. I remember the years of my training and early nursing career so vividly. These stories have been enjoyed by others, over many years, and are now captured in this book. I have written more stories, following my marriage in 1963, and I hope to share them too.

So much has changed in nursing, but the need for compassion and respect has not. I hope that any younger reader, who may be considering nursing as a career, will be inspired by these stories to follow their vocation and remember to treat patients with the kindness they deserve – as if they were beloved family or friends.

Jeanie Traynor Maltby (née Shaw)